Follow
Your Star

Follow Your Star

CAREER LESSONS I LEARNED FROM MOM

Kristin Sherry

PRAISE FOR *FOLLOW YOUR STAR*

"Kristin Sherry has woven together beautifully told, true stories and powerful, compelling career insights to illuminate what everyone needs to really know and follow into this wonderful book. Filled with magical moments and important and inspiring information, this is a great guide to successfully following your star to career fulfillment and success. Highly recommended!"

Steve Lishansky
Author, *The Ultimate Sales Revolution* & President, Optimize International

"This is a must read! With Follow Your Star, Kristin has struck a rare balance between the inspiration, encouragement and readability that only comes from storytelling, and the hard-hitting impact that comes from research and analysis."

John Freeze
Author, *Straighten the Path* & Executive Director, Crossroads Career Network

"Follow Your Star is impressive! It's clean, clear, and simple, and is filled with strategic principles and practical tools. This book about careers is a unique combination of information, inspiration, and application that equals transformation!"

Brian Ray
Author, *Created for Good Works*

"*Follow Your Star* is the most comprehensive path for discovering your talents. The simple yet thought-provoking concepts in this book are perfect for anyone searching for complete fulfillment in their work."

Amy Pearl
Co-Author, *The Collaboration Breakthrough* & President, RV Rhodes, LLC

"Packed with practical tips and peppered with wit and wisdom, this book is a solid roadmap to chart your career course!"

Susan Whitcomb
Author of 7 Career Books & Founder/President,
TheAcademies.com

"A priceless resource that demystifies the science and art of self-discovery. Follow Your Star generously shares with the reader a thoughtful and proven protocol to uncover your unique self and take the steps to find professional and personal fulfillment. With the sensitivity of a great coach, Kristin poses challenging and thought-provoking questions and shares personal stories of ob-stacles and triumph to guide you through 5 key phases to unravel the twists and turns of your own professional journey. Unlike the traditional textbook self-help guide, Follow Your Star reads like a conversation - carry your own personal coach with you and un-derstand the tools and steps you will need to transform your life."

Laura Casoni
Director, Workforce Development Services, Goodwill Industries
of the Southern Piedmont

For my father, Wayne W. Spear,
A rock of responsibility,
A man of integrity,
And the best dad I could ever have.
You've contributed more to my personal
and professional success than you'll ever know.

Table of Contents

Foreword

by my brother,
WAYNE K. SPEAR

What I've Learned by Looking at Trees

"HAVE YOU EVER WONDERED, as I did recently, what determines the seemingly random pattern of tree branches?

A case of 'every which way,' it appears. One branch projects confidently toward the sky—another launches tentatively in one direction, suddenly adopting a new trajectory.

A life is the same.

I know this, because I can see my own life in these branches. That little ragged outgrowth that goes nowhere? That's a girl I dated in high school. The long, straight branch which stops suddenly? An office job I once had. The fat branch with many small off-shoots? My writing career. The trunk? That represents my up-bringing: the formative experiences which established my values, outlook, and dreams.

To this day, my trunk is nourishing the new branches which sprout in my life.

I noticed that there are a lot of dead-ends on a tree: but look at those branches, and you'll see many outgrowths. Again, I think of the times I've come to the end of a path. Maybe it was a goal I didn't reach, or a job I didn't get.

When you're standing at the end of a path you thought and hoped would go farther, you only see losses and failures—the job you didn't get, the money you won't make, and the things you won't be able to do and have because you won't get that pay check.

Looking back, you can see that those endings are in fact launching points, like new shoots from a branch. My first business, which I created in high school, was the result of having the doors to gainful employment shut in my face. Within a month, I had more business than I could manage. I made more money and was far happier than I would have been in a job, but I felt depressed and defeated all the same when my plan to be hired by someone else didn't work out.

What I learned by looking at trees is that you can reverse engineer the process, applying it to your future. You can look forward as well as back. Today I see 'dead-ends' and 'failures' as intrinsic to the organic process of creating a path of your own.

A tree is the sum total of its experiments in reaching the light, and rarely (if ever) is this effort a straight line from vision to reality. We humans, however, seem to be addicted to the idea that life works (or at least should work) as follows:

Aspirations —> A Well-Laid Plan —> Goal Achieved!

I know this kind of thinking has often been applied by me. Many times, I've been disappointed and discouraged because I haven't been able to draw, and then pursue, a straight line from Point A to Point B. Even when I've 'known' life is more complicated than that, I've acted as if it weren't.

The prime directive of a tree is to reach the life-giving light. All that apparently crazy, here-there-and-everywhere is in service of the tree's need for sun. And that's why I've changed my thinking, as well as my way of creating a path.

You see, the tree is on to something—and I think I know what it is.

I'm not talking about creating 10 new businesses or launching 50 new projects. I'm not suggesting you should run, willy-nilly, in every direction. That's certainly not what I do. Instead, I focus on activating as many potential trajectories in my life as I can, by nourishing relationships in my life and business. Just as the prime directive of a tree is to reach the life-giving light, my prime directive is to nurture my community, every day.

The second thing I do is to introduce as much variety into my life as I can. I take long showers. I go for walks in the woods. I meet with, and talk to, as many interesting people as I can. When I really need to be productive, I get away from my desk.

Because here is the worst way I've found to be productive:

Sit at Computer —> Work Eight Hours —> Get Results

And yet that's still how we see work, as a linear process.

The fact is that we are addicted to straight lines and old ways of doing things. I know how hard it is to let go. I've made painful adjustments. I used to believe in things like:

Go to School —> Get an Education —> Work Hard —> Succeed

or

Get an Agent —> Find a Publisher —> Write Books —> Make Money or

Get Hired by a Newspaper —> File Stories —> Get Paid
—> Retire

None of these things have worked out as advertised. I've only been miserable and unfulfilled pursuing them. It took a painful adjustment, and months of study and effort, to let go of the old ways of thinking. And that was after years of emotional work, gradually getting to the place where I could admit that what I was doing wasn't working—and would never work.

Going in a new direction is hard. You may have a decade invested in that branch of yours. It may be the favorite branch on your tree. Maybe it's the only branch. You probably imagined it soaring one day above the canopy, into the full and glorious life-affirming sun of a new day. But what if it doesn't?

If you build your life on the principle of abundance, each day nurturing a wide network of relationships, being open to many possibilities—sending out many branches—you'll never have this problem. You'll soon realize that your life is, like a tree, the sum total of its trajectories, explorations, and so-called 'dead-ends.'

A tree, like a life, is nothing less than the sum of its experiments."

PART 1

Mom's Story

This book begins with the true story of my mom, Judi, and shares what I've learned from watching her find and follow her star.

Through her story, I will characterize five specific success strategies she employed and provide you with key principles you can apply to your own career. You can achieve maximum leadership, career, and personal potential by investing in the five key areas that are correlated to career success for women.

The insights you will gain from this book will provide valuable awareness and tangible ways you can move in a positive direction, both personally and professionally. And that direction will put you on the path to maximum fulfillment, regardless of the stage of your life.

Judi Johns was born into a poor Native American family in 1945, the youngest of nine children. Judi was a bright girl but small town high school life bored her. She dropped out at the beginning of her senior year, and soon afterwards married her high school sweetheart.

At age 18, Judi's husband, Wayne, joined the police force. They rented a tiny house which they affectionately referred to as the Kleenex® Box, because it was similarly shaped and not a great deal bigger. The Kleenex® Box was situated on a rural road, right in the middle of nowhere. It was located next to a rock quarry that spewed dust into the house when the windows were left open.

Their son Wayne was born when Judi was 20. Almost six years later the family was complete with my birth.

Judi began adult life the way many young women did in the 1960s – a stay-at-home mom who didn't possess a high school diploma or a driver's license.

By the time my brother and I were both in school full-time, my mother had done seamstress work at home for 12 years and she was restless. Judi wanted to do something different with her life, including having a career outside of the home.

> "I was tired of being at home, and I felt helpless; I wanted to have my own money. I think I just wanted more control over my life – except I didn't really have any skills or education."

Once she determined she wanted to work outside the home, Judi began thinking of ways she might enter the workforce. With little education and limited work experience, her choices were few. She did, however, have some options.

What strategies did Judi employ to find and attain a fulfilling and successful career? She began by leveraging the sewing skills she developed during the 12 years she spent working at home. She had done seamstress work for a woman who worked at Peace Bridge Brokerage, a freight forwarding company. Later, when the company needed uniforms for some of the women, they called Judi to make them.

> "I had done sewing for PBB. They knew I was a hard worker so I thought they might hire me to do something

else for them. I applied for a job and two weeks later they hired me as a receptionist. I was a sponge. I was happy to learn anything they would teach me. It was the very beginning of computers, but there was electronic equipment and I wanted to learn it all!

I found it interesting that the executives would come and talk to me at reception. Years later I realized they came to me because of my Strategic strength. That was the beginning of the realization I could coach people.

Three significant things happened to me while I was at PBB:

First, an executive mentioned he didn't like using a Dictaphone. I signed up for a night school class and learned shorthand. I went to him and told him he didn't have to use the Dictaphone anymore; just tell me, I'll write it in shorthand. He liked the way I reworded things he would say, because he thought I said it better.

Shortly after that, he was promoted and was allowed to have his own secretary, and he asked for me. Once I was in that role he asked me if I could help the purchasing department. He said it wasn't working the way it should, so they sent me to help purchasing to get more organized.

Second, about a year later, the president came to me and said, 'We don't have a personnel department – we have information. I'd like you to get all of our data organized so we can create a personnel department.'

I had access to all the confidential information. I noticed people's experience levels and how much they were paid. I thought to myself, 'None of these people are any smarter than me, and they don't work much harder.' I noticed they had more experience and more education. It said to me, 'You need to get more education in a field that interests you if you want to make more money.'

I had always been interested in how people tick and how organizations function. The year I was expecting [my daughter], I remember reading *Up the Organization*, by Robert Townsend. I went to the library all the time with my husband. I was a stay-at-home mom, a high school dropout, and here I am, reading a book on Organizational Development in my sister Rhoda's pool! So when I was given the chance to do these things at the Brokerage, it was all the things I was interested in. My strengths are in people and data.

Those experiences at the Brokerage showed me I had a future. They were pivotal moments: Executives finding value in talking to me, working on projects with significant outcomes, and the realization that I needed an education, and I needed it quickly.

At that time, PBB was a defensive culture, and it laid the foundation for me creating the culture pyramid that has now turned into a book.

I thought to myself, 'You can do more.' I talked to my sister Joan about it, and she encouraged me and said, 'You should quit your job.' And so I did.

After quitting my job, I went to Brock University and walked into the business department. There was an adjunct professor of accounting there, and he said he would meet with me. I asked him what I needed to do to get into school. I told him what I wanted to do and after I babbled away for a while, he asked me, 'How long has it been since you've been in school full time?'

I was 34, and it was 17 years since I quit high school. So, 17 years. He said, 'You're too old to go to school full-time.' I wanted to burst into tears! He said to me, 'Here's what I think you should do: Go look for a job in a field that interests you and go to school part-time, at night.'

I wanted to go to work for a CEO or an executive, and be their right hand as an Executive Assistant. I thought if I could do that, I'd be happy doing that for the rest of my life!

I started reading the *Buffalo News* because I knew there wasn't a job like that in Fort Erie. I interviewed for six jobs, and was offered five of them.

I talked to my mother to get her opinion on which job I should take. She said, 'Take the job at Westwood Pharmaceuticals [a division of Bristol-Myers Squibb]. People will always need food and drugs.' My mother was always so wise.

I had gone for the interview on a Thursday at Westwood Pharmaceuticals. It was a behavior-based interview. Vic Davis, the Vice President of HR, had been using temp agency secretaries since April. It was now September and he was totally fed up. I told him I wanted to get into management and that I wasn't looking for a job, I was looking for a career. I wasn't home an hour and they called and offered me the job.

September 15, 1980 was my first day [at Westwood Pharmaceuticals], and I went to my first university class two days later. I spent an hour with the Director of Recruiting and half a day with my new boss, Vic. He explained the role he was playing and how I would help him. Have you ever heard of a Vice President spending a half-day with their admin?

Every day I worked really hard. I wanted to impress my boss, and I learned everything I could. I showed up early and did my very best every day. Anything they wanted me to learn, I was interested in learning.

While I worked for Vic, he made the comment, 'Everyone that comes here for a meeting comments on you; how well you represent me, what a great personality you have, how competent you are.'

Vic gave me feedback like that regularly. He also gave me feedback when I did something that was *not* worthy of my ability. Thank God I was receptive to that feedback! I listened, and I learned.

Vic allowed me to read everything that came across his desk. That was back in the days when a lot of things were still on paper. It gave me a bird's eye view into how organizations work, and I began to see opportunities.

After about two and a half years, I knew the president was so unhappy with the weekly company newsletter that came out. He would write notes on it and put it in Vic's mailbox. The one that tipped the scales for me was when it showed up in Vic's inbox and the President had written one word on it: **'UGH!'**

I knew the newsletter had hit rock bottom. So I went to Vic and I told him what I thought was wrong with the newsletter. I told him it had no identity tied to what was important to the company. It had no personality. It's not teaching employees anything, or giving people anything to think about.

Then I asked him 'Why don't you let me be the editor?' He asked me to write a proposal, but I had no idea how to write one. I had never written a proposal before, so I just threw some words on paper. They gave it to me, and I transformed it."

Persuading her manager and the president to allow her to take on the company newsletter, eventually took Judi down a path that led to a role as Key Manager, Corporate Communications.

When I was 9, my mother was working during the day and she pursued a double major in Business and English Literature in the evenings. She was always reading, so my dad made my lunches before he went to work, and prepared dinner on the evenings mom was in school. I still remember notes of wisdom he'd leave in my school lunch bag: "Don't wipe your nose on your sleeve."

My mother often joked that if she fell off the face of the earth my dad could keep everything running like a well-oiled machine.

She wasn't quite joking, because he knew our schedules and how to run a household, unlike many men from the baby boomer generation.

Even though this story focuses on the career lessons learned from my mom, make no mistake, this story couldn't have been told were it not for my dad.

I remember my parents would sit in companion wing-back chairs after dinner and on the weekends, reading. Most of mom's evenings would end around 8:00 p.m., sitting on the couch with her eyes closed and a book in her hands.

When I'd ask, "Mom, are you asleep?" she would respond in sleepy, slurred speech, "I'm just resting my eyes." Finally, my dad would say, "Judi. Jude? Judi! Come on. Let's go to bed."

Our house was often quiet because everyone had their faces in books. We had books all over the house; in shelves, on every table surface, in baskets and boxes. They were everywhere, and covered a wide variety of topics. Mom often cited facts and quotations, or shared interesting anecdotes from books she was reading.

Judi recalls:

"My grandmother used to scold me when I was a little girl. She told me I was nosy and asked too many questions.

Early in my career I had no confidence. I felt the need to show I was smart and it got me into trouble. I was waiting for people to tell me, and so it went to my head when Vic treated me like I was smart, and I got pushy. The other secretaries didn't like me. I worked through lunch instead of eating with them in the lunch room. I looked *up*. I cared about what executives thought.

It didn't change until I was a senior manager and I was put on a taskforce with people who worked on the line. I thought, "What am I doing here with people who work in production?" That experience taught me to be respectful of people regardless of what they do. I found out the best use of my time was to understand these people and help them solve their problems. I was ashamed of myself; I was a snob. I met so many great people who worked in production, and if they knew what I had thought they'd have shunned me, and I would have deserved it.

At Westwood, I had the good fortune to be surrounded by smart, nice people. It was a culture that demanded those two things of people. I learned what an emotionally intelligent culture looks like.

That guy that said come to school at night? That turned out to be brilliant advice. Everything I learned I got to immediately apply. My boss would say, 'Okay, that's the theory, here's what happens in the real world.' It put my education on steroids. Because I'm so flexible and open to opportunities, I kept saying, 'OK, I'll try that.'

With all of the changes taking place, I knew we were being chipped away at; parts of our business were being moved. I could see my job going to New Jersey–except I couldn't go to New Jersey.

In 1996, I went to the Center for Creative Leadership and when I got there and experienced it, I said, 'This is what I need to do: help people figure out who they are, and what they need to be successful.'

When I came back I went to the Jewish Family Center for career counseling and they put me through assessments. Every week I showed my boss what I had learned about myself. After the second week my boss said, 'We're going to pay for this.'

Within three months of returning from the Center for Creative Leadership, I resigned. It was time for me to strike out on my own. I did it without researching, or talking to other consultants. I was so ill-prepared it wasn't funny.

At the time, I was working on a big project at Westwood and was managing the communication for an inactive hazardous waste site clean-up, and it was very complicated. I was the finger on the pulse in the city.

The lawyers in New York did not want a new person taking it over and told my boss, 'You have to give her a contract. And it has to be for at least a year.' That contract gave me money while I started my business."

Today, Judi is the founder of RV Rhodes, a successful firm of coaches and organizational development professionals who provide strategic solutions and tools to organizations to help them achieve their workforce goals. She has coached more than 40,000 people, largely CEOs and executives, and worked with over 100 companies ranging in revenues from 10 million to multiple billions.

A strong desire for meaningful work is seeded within the human soul. Every woman is wired differently and while some women achieve fulfillment at home, others feel something is missing in their lives. Your choices are personal, and each has its own benefits.

Ultimately this book is not about following Judi's path from high school dropout to CEO. It's about reaching your own personal and professional potential. It's about how to invest in areas correlated to success, to help you crush obstacles, and stand out from the crowd as a result.

Like Judi, you may feel something is missing in your life. Perhaps you want to move to the next step in your career, but you feel stuck. Maybe you're contemplating re-entry into the workforce after an extended period in the home. Or it could be you woke up one day and realized where you are right now is not where you're meant to be.

I'd like to help you course-correct your journey to become the person you are meant to be in full measure—which takes informed, determined, intentional steps. This book will provide the guidance you need to determine what those steps are, and how to take them.

Before we dive into the five success strategies, we're going to take a self-discovery detour. If you're crystal clear on your career path, and have found work that sustains and energizes you, feel free to skip ahead to Part 3: The Five Success Strategies.

Are you ready? Let's begin!

PART 2

First Things First

Why You're Here

Life's too short to spend doing work that isn't fulfilling. A picture is worth a thousand words:

Figure 1a

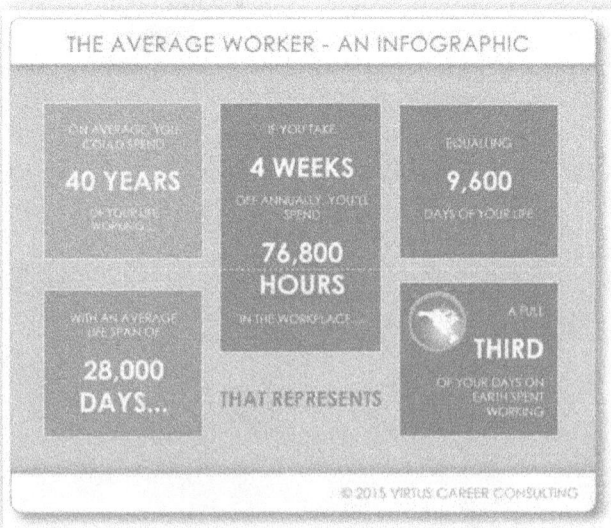

THE AVERAGE WORKER - AN INFOGRAPHIC

ON AVERAGE, YOU COULD SPEND
40 YEARS
OF YOUR LIFE WORKING...

IF YOU TAKE
4 WEEKS
OFF ANNUALLY, YOU'LL SPEND
76,800 HOURS
IN THE WORKPLACE...

EQUALLING
9,600
DAYS OF YOUR LIFE

WITH AN AVERAGE LIFE SPAN OF
28,000 DAYS...

THAT REPRESENTS

A FULL
THIRD
OF YOUR DAYS ON EARTH SPENT WORKING

© 2015 VIRTUS CAREER CONSULTING

This book is not about what you're capable of today. To move toward career fulfillment, it's necessary to determine where you are, and discover where you want to be. The gap between those two points is your potential.

Potential is defined as having or showing the capacity to become or develop into something *in the future.*

Many people – including a good number of my clients – feel stuck. Some of them can't see the forest for the trees with respect to their next career step. They're often too close to themselves and identifying the perfect career overwhelms them.

Are you thriving on autopilot, or withering a little more inside with each passing day?

The first step you should take when contemplating your career vision is to assess where you currently are on a Career Satisfaction Continuum (*Figure 1b*). Career *dissatisfaction* is represented at the left of the continuum, and career *fulfillment* is on the right.

Figure 1b

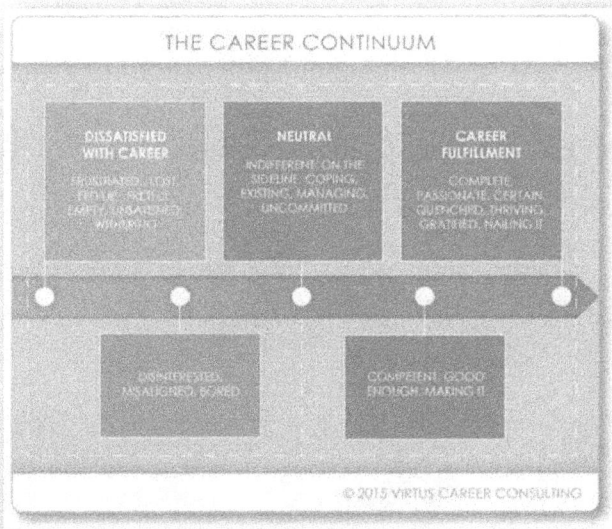

If you're on the far right of the continuum, congratulations! There are many statistics related to career satisfaction, and most sources agree the majority of working adults are dissatisfied. A 2013 Gallup poll revealed only 13% of adults report being engaged at work, worldwide.[1]

According to a 2009 study released by the National Bureau of Economics, women reported the lowest levels of happiness in almost 35 years.[2] Perhaps we feel we need to be successful in more domains than ever, whether it's caring for aging parents, raising children, maintaining healthy relationships, contributing to the household finances, or juggling domestic responsibilities.

Oftentimes, when my clients talk to me about their dissatisfaction with their career, they give examples of what they dislike about their present circumstances, but struggle to pinpoint the root of their dissatisfaction.

They may tell me they're unhappy with their job because they're stuck in an office looking at spreadsheets all day, instead of interacting with other people. However, people are a means to an end. That may sound cold, but what I mean is, *what need does that actually fulfill?*

If you have unfulfilled career needs, it's my hope that by the time you've finished reading this book, you'll not only be inspired but you will have a clearer picture of what your specific needs are, and have the tools and resources you need to pursue them.

Career Patterns

Our personalities and preferences strongly influence the type of career pattern we gravitate toward, and the good news is, there are perfectly valid career patterns that are often forgotten, over-looked, or simply unknown.

The main career patterns are:

Vertical Career Pattern

For most people, thinking about their career path brings to mind the concept of a traditional, vertical pattern. In general, people who are motivated by power, responsibility, external rewards, and increasingly visible achievement follow this pattern.

Expert Career Pattern

The expert desires to delve deeper into an area of expertise, to become a knowledgeable and respected subject matter expert in their field. Expert careerists are also known as *Specialists* and tend to be motivated by stability, status, authority, or competence.

Spiral Career Pattern

The career "spiraler" becomes bored performing the same job for more than a couple of years – or however long it takes to exhaust the opportunities in their role. These 'job hoppers' are personally motivated by growth and learning. Due to their broad skill base, they are often *Generalists* who are able to pursue a wide range of roles. Spiralers tend to make several lateral career moves that lead to a continual increase in their skill set.

Independent Career Pattern

Independents resist being employees. They are motivated by autonomy, flexibility, and variety. These careerists often become independent contractors, entrepreneurs, solopreneurs, business owners, and consultants.

It's important to note that not everyone wants a vertical, accelerated climb up the career ladder. That wasn't what I wanted, so I understand this all too well. If you aren't a ladder climber, discard the notion you must follow that path! You can embrace your natural tendencies and still achieve career fulfillment.

On more than one occasion, I thought something was surely wrong with me because I couldn't stay in one lane for more than two or three years. I wondered why I didn't want to stick with a particular career long enough to climb the ladder in one functional area.

In hindsight, moving across industries and functional areas was the best foundation I could have laid to better serve my clients as a Career and Executive Coach. For the majority of my career, I followed the spiral pattern. My career path moved from Education to Information Technology to Reporting. I went on to roles in Operations, Learning & Development and ultimately, Career and Executive Coaching. In recent years, I've moved into professional speaking and now writing.

Before you can follow your star, you may need helping finding it. Regardless of your career pattern tendencies, the five key factors for success I present in this book are applicable to achieving your potential. Get ready to roll up your sleeves!

Find Your Star

People are multifaceted and complex, and we hold deep biases and blind spots about ourselves.

The more sources you use to increase your self-knowledge, the better. Lombardo & Eichinger (2003) found in 360 evaluations – a feedback process which includes direct feedback from subordinates, peers, and supervisors, as well as self-evaluation – the *self*-rating tends to be the *least* accurate.

The boss rating tends to be the *most* accurate.[3] Looking at the average rating across all 360 surveys, the boss is the closest to the average rating while the self-rater has the greatest deviation from it. In other words, you are most off the mark when it comes to rating your performance!

Valerie McMurray, Principal of NorthStar Consulting Group, has years of experience in leadership research and working with clients in executive coaching, which led to the development of the Women's Inventory of Success Empowerment (WISE) Profile, a powerful behavioral assessment specifically for women that measures career and leadership success factors.

According to McMurray, to become more self-aware, we must "combine candid feedback and the opinions of others with self-learning in an introspective process that leads to conscious knowledge and understanding of one's own behaviors, feelings, motives, character, values and goals – working on areas that need improvement through reflection and understanding."

Back in 2012, while obtaining my WorkPlace Big Five certification from RV Rhodes, I was introduced to a concept they developed known as the Human Iceberg.

Amy Pearl, the president of RV Rhodes, explained that people are like icebergs. About 15% of an iceberg is typically seen above the surface of the water; the rest lies beneath the surface.

In people, what we see on the surface are *behaviors*. Yet there are multiple factors beneath the surface which influence how someone behaves, the preferences they have, and why they think and feel the way they do.

This graphic visually demonstrates some of the elements of our unique makeup that lie beneath the surface.

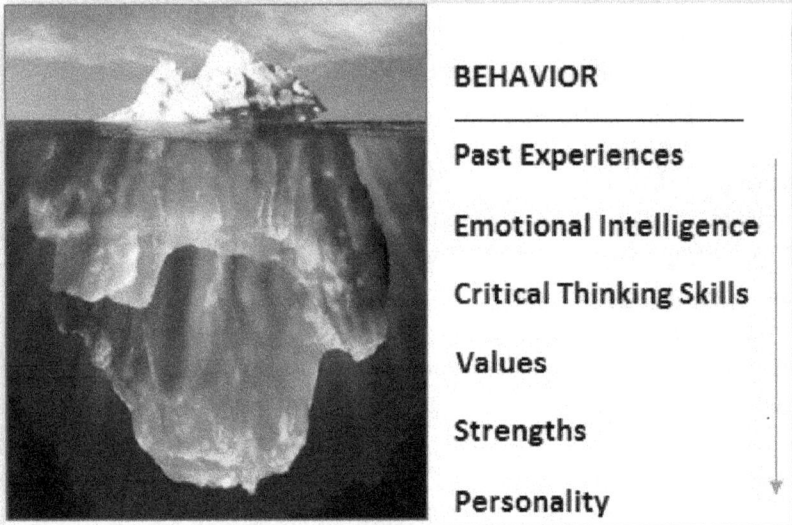

BEHAVIOR

Past Experiences

Emotional Intelligence

Critical Thinking Skills

Values

Strengths

Personality

The elements at the base of the iceberg (personality and strengths) are innate; these characteristics are a part of us that is inborn, inherited from our parents.

As we move upward toward the surface, these elements of our makeup are more subject to influence by our environment. Past experiences, emotional intelligence, critical thinking skills, our values, strengths – or natural talents, and personality all work together to influence who we are. These elements weave a complex tapestry, contributing to our God-given uniqueness and influence the behavior seen by others, in other words, what is observable on the surface.

If you want to find and follow your star, you must investigate these layers beneath the surface. A clearer picture of who you are and what motivates you emerges, which enables you to pursue a path that brings increased fulfillment in every area of your life.

It can be overwhelming, exciting, and sometimes painful to delve beneath the surface. This is why I often introduce myself as a career guide rather than a coach, because navigating your career is a journey, and I function as a Sherpa to my clients on that journey.

I suggest everyone revisit the process of exploration more than once in their lives, because the factors beneath the surface of the iceberg change over time.

Your personality is influenced by new skills, experiences, and environmental variations, which is why some expressions of our personality change over the course of our lives, while other aspects of our personality remain virtually unchanged.

When working with clients on career discovery, I start at the bottom of their iceberg and work upward, one layer at a time. So let's take a look at each factor in your unique makeup, and consider how you might use this information for your own career discovery. We'll also follow the career discovery of a real client case study that illustrates how this knowledge can be practically applied.

As I mentioned, your personality is found at the base of the iceberg and it is the foundation of what makes you, you; it's a logical starting point in the process to understand your temperament and motivations, and the priorities that are rooted there.

These motivations and priorities have tremendous influence on your interpersonal effectiveness as well as your career choice. I can't tell you how many times I've met people who prioritize collaboration and teamwork, yet they spend every day working miserably behind a computer screen, with little interpersonal interaction.

Conversely, people who prioritize results-driven, task-oriented work are likely to experience the phenomena known as Death by Meeting, characterized by author Patrick Lencioni:

"There are two basic problems. First, meetings lack drama. Which means they are boring. Second, most meetings lack context and purpose. They are a confusing mix of administrivia, tactics, strategy and review, all of which creates unfocused, meandering and seemingly endless conferences, with little resolution or clarity."

You can see why result-focused, task-oriented people would find this frustrating!

Your vision, your values
One of the United States of America's Founding Fathers, Benjamin Franklin, once wrote:
"There are three things extremely hard – steel, a diamond, and to know one's self."
Knowing this, it's quite challenging for many people to think creatively about what career opportunities are not only available to them, but best for them.
Before we move forward, ask yourself: *What is my vision of the future for my career?*
Put simply, your vision is what you hope to achieve; something you imagine. More often than not, a person's core values are neglected in some way when they are dissatisfied with their career. The same holds true for one's personal life.
Despite this, people rarely spend time figuring out exactly what is most important to them and are destined to continually make decisions that are not aligned with their values, making

career satisfaction and a vision for the future an ever-elusive prospect.

This happens because people tend to evaluate their next opportunity using a narrow set of factors, such as company perks, benefits, and work tasks, instead of making strategic choices based on what they *value* most.

I have many clients who first came to me indicating they wanted to transition careers so they could work more with people. In many cases their jobs were very administrative, or task-oriented. In each client, what they needed and what they valued were very different.

For example, one client didn't just want to work with people, she wanted regular interactions with *different* people. She wasn't looking to build close connections with a small team of five people. She loved the thrill of making new acquaintances. In fact, the idea of working with the same group day after day repelled her.

This was not made clear until we dug a little deeper together, but the distinction made all the difference in the world. There are different needs and values underlying the desire to work closely with the same group, versus meeting new people on a daily basis.

Few things can rob your joy like not being true to yourself, or not upholding what you believe. Knowing what you value is the key to unlocking answers that will guide you to ultimate career satisfaction!

Simply put, your values are your judgment of what's important to you in life; a measure of what ought to be. Because they're what you deem most important, they set your priorities and are therefore a good measure if your life is moving in the direction you want – one that is aligned to what you value most.

Why are values so important? Your values are the easiest and most direct access point to discovering your identity! It's less likely you will achieve life and career fulfillment without knowing your identity.

If you're working in a job where your company is asking you to withhold information, sell things to customers that they don't need, suppress who you are, or keep silent on your values, you will be continuously drained by the emotional energy required to live a dual life.

Unlike our personality and strengths, we are not born with our values. Values are shaped over our lifetime and are heavily influenced by our experiences, belief systems, the people in our lives and yes, to some extent by our personality.

Many people struggle to know or articulate their values beyond moral beliefs, such as honesty and fairness. Intentionally examining your values is critically important, but it's an exercise few people actively undertake.

The Values Identification Process

The first step in identifying your values is to think about what's most important to you. As you do this, it's important to recognize the difference between an *end* and a *means to an end*.

For example, you might say, "My family is most important to me." Your family is a *means to an end*. You can value them, but your family is not a value.

To get to a value, ask yourself, "What is it *about* my family that's most important to me?"

You might answer, "Spending time together." Well, spending time is an activity, not a value, so you must then ask, "What does spending time with my family give me?"

The answer might be love and connection with other people. See how that works? The family is a means to an end. The end is *love and connection with others.*

I will be forever grateful to my mentor, Steve Lishansky, for teaching me this distinction.

Allow me to share a personal example to illustrate this point. Knowing my values has allowed me to evaluate personal and professional decisions to ensure I don't wind up in deeply dissatisfying situations. My current career is the best fit I've ever experienced, because my work satisfies my values.

I realized a key aspect about myself early in my career: as long as I was a traditional employee, my strong need for autonomy was likely to be neglected. This led me to acknowledge working for myself was truly a prerequisite to ultimate career satisfaction; therefore, every career decision I made from that point forward was made through the lens of that vision of my future to increase the likelihood of achieving the end goal of being self-employed.

Would you like to discover your values? Download this values exercise from my website: *http://virtuscareers.com/Documents/ Follow%20Your%20Star/Identifying%20Your%20Values.pdf*

In 2015, my mentor guided me through an eye-opening, life-changing exercise of discovering and prioritizing my values. They are, in order:

- *Love and connection* – maintaining healthy relationships with people
- *Making a contribution* – my work has to make a difference to the people I'm serving
- *Autonomy* – a strong desire to self-govern; freedom from being controlled by others
- *Having fun* – work hard, play just as hard

- *Challenge* – work that is not boring, and involves overcoming complexity to achieve success
- *Variety* – the people I engage with, and the tasks and services I perform
- *Learning and growth* – consistent acquisition of new skills and knowledge
- *Accomplishment* – tangible achievements experienced on a regular basis

How does a prioritized list of values help you?

Sometimes you must make a difficult or important decision (e.g. whether to accept a job offer), and because all your values might not be able to be satisfied you need to know what's *most* important to you.

Explicitly knowing what you value will improve your track record of making decisions that are right for you. Remember this if you ask for others' opinions on a decision you will make: their advice might work well for some, but only if they share your values.

When I know what I value and prioritize, it allows me to live a life aligned to those values. When my life aligns to my values, the more fulfilled and productive I become.

Let's look at an example:

My top value is *Love and connection*, but I also strongly value *Contribution* (to others). If I were presented an opportunity to have all the *Contribution* I could ever want, but I couldn't have *Love and connection* (let's say it required me to be away from my loved ones much of the time), my number one value will be violated because I would be separated from those I am most connected to, particularly my husband and children. Such a decision would be much more difficult if I didn't know my prioritized values.

Because I know my most important value, I don't accept opportunities that would require frequent or extended travel that would separate me from my loved ones. Decision-making is simple for me, no matter how attractive an opportunity may be. Does it violate my most important priorities? If yes, the answer has to be "no" if I'm going to live a fulfilled life.

Also, because I know *Love and connection* is my most important value, I build a connection with people I serve in a coaching capacity. It is not uncommon for my clients to want to have some level of continued contact with me after an engagement because of the bond we form. They know I care about their success and well-being, and at the end of our engagement there is often a feeling of loss that we'll no longer be working together. I found that interesting when I first started my practice, but revealing my values helped me understand why this happens.

Prioritizing Your Values

Once you have your list of values, prioritize them by reflecting on this question:

If I could have all the *Value A* I want, but I could never have *Value B*, which would I choose?

You're likely to have an emotional response when faced with a forced choice. Pay attention to your gut reaction to the question. It's yielding your answer!

I have a client who worked as a Marketing Manager for eight years. In 2013, she quit her job and has since been working temporary jobs while trying to figure out her next steps.

When I spoke with her and uncovered her abilities and strengths, everything seemed to suggest a strong fit with her last role, so I began to dig a bit deeper and share insights about how she is wired. The light bulb went on for her.

She shared that for the past three years, she was miserable in her role but she didn't know why. After exploring her values and strengths, two factors emerged: shady ethics in the company's culture and having to influence those over whom she had no authority. Why should those points bother her? Ethics were important to her because *Integrity* was her strongest value; she found *Influencing without Authority* to be draining.

This was a significant breakthrough for my client. She realized she *does* love marketing, but she also needs to work in an organizational culture and within a structure that doesn't conflict with her values and preferences.

What's your most important value? Are you living your life in alignment with that value? If you're not fulfilled, this is a great starting place to find out why.

The Four Personality Characteristics: DiSC
There are a number of models to describe personality. Everything DiSC® by Wiley is among the most well-known. Let's spend a few minutes looking at how this model explains the characteristics, needs, and motivations through four personality styles:

Dominance (D)
Dominance, or D, denotes a strong personality. These task-oriented, decisive people focus on results and the big picture. They are fast-paced multi-taskers. Ds are often verbal, take-charge people.

Ds enjoy leading others; many people leaders are primary or secondary *Ds.* This style thrives in fast-paced environments that value action, results, and challenging the status quo. Two-thirds of leaders in the corporate environment have dominance as a primary or secondary personality style. Donald Trump is dominance-driven, so was Steve Jobs.

Influence (I)

Influence, or *I*, are also big picture, fast-paced, multi-tasking, and verbal people. The core difference is that *I*s are relationship-oriented, not task-oriented. Is are enthusiastic, energetic, and inspirational. They want to be liked, and appreciate recognition.

*I*s enjoy working with a variety of different people. *I*s are satisfied when their jobs provide recognition and reward, have variety, and the opportunity to manage relationships and influence others, such as sales, training, speaking, or consulting. *I*s often gravitate toward fields that are based on working with people, such as sales, consulting, training, and marketing. Jay Leno is an *I*, so was Robin Williams.

Steadiness (S)

Steadiness, or *S*, is similar to *I* in being relationship-oriented. They differ from the *I* in being calmer and less verbal. Steadfast personalities are opposite to *D*s. *S*s work linearly, at a more moderate pace. They are loyal, good listeners who express warmth and friendliness.

*S*s like working with a team, and building authentic, strong, and supportive work relationships. They gravitate to roles such as teaching, counseling, administrative support, or social work. Their work style is methodical and detail-oriented; they do not multi-task. *S*s often seek work helping others, such as jobs in the non-profit sector, teaching, and counseling. Mother Teresa and Mr. Rogers were *Ss*.

Conscientiousness (C)

Conscientious, or *Cs*, are detail-oriented, (versus big picture *D* and *I*). *Cs* have a reserved temperament: they are process-oriented, valuing stability. However, *Cs* differ from *Ss* in that they are task-oriented, rather than relationship-oriented.

Cs enjoy work that requires attention to detail, quality, accuracy, and logic. Because they are task-oriented, *Cs* are often found in technology, engineering, quality, and compliance. Bill Gates is a *C*, so was Albert Einstein.

Interactions between DiSC Styles

It's important to note 85% of people have a blend of two personality styles; only 15% of the population have only one. A person's secondary personality trait strongly influences their personality.

Have you noticed the similarities between individual styles? It often happens that a priority straddles two quadrants of the circle (Figure 1c). It is the overlap between styles that creates common ground:

Ds and *Is* prioritize *action*

Is and *Ss* prioritize *collaboration*

Cs and *Ss* prioritize *stability*

Ds and *Cs* prioritize *challenge*

Ds and *Ss* do not share common priorities, nor do *Is* and *Cs*. These personality combinations may be prone to greater friction and have more difficulty understanding each other.

Figure 1c

Attributes of the Styles

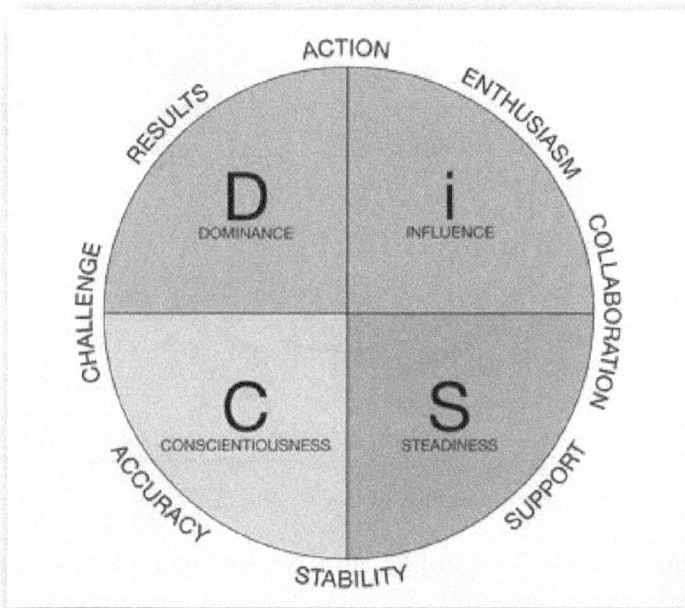

What's my DiSC style?
Let me share a simple technique that will help you identify your personality style, and the primary style of others.

1. Are you *fast-paced and outspoken* **OR** *cautious and reflective?*
2. Are you *questioning and skeptical* **OR** *accepting and warm?*

3. Combine your answers to questions 1 and 2 to discover your style. For example, if you said *fast-paced and outspoken + accepting and warm,* your primary style is *I*.

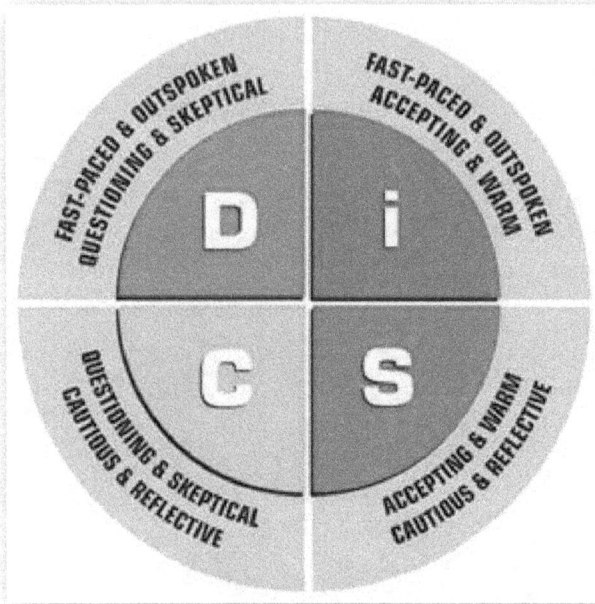

©2012 John Wiley & Sons, Inc.

Remember most people have a primary and a secondary style, so you may identify with more than one trait, and your secondary style will influence your primary style. For example, if you are primarily a *D*, but your secondary style is *I*, you will be more relationship-oriented than a pure *D*, or a *DC*, i.e., a *D* with a secondary style of *C*. In fact, you're likely to switch between task and relationship orientation, depending on the situation.

In summary, *Ds* and *Cs* are task-oriented, while *Is* and *Ss* are relationship-oriented. *Ds* and *Is* are fast-paced, big picture thinkers. *Cs* and *Ss* are detail-oriented and like to work at a moderate pace.

Invest in Yourself: DiSC Personality Assessment
Are you interested in learning more about Everything DiSC®? If you're interested in an assessment and personalized coaching about motivators, stressors, and strategies for increased effectiveness, please contact me through my website, *www.virtuscareers. com.*

Strengths
It's time to move to the next layer of the iceberg, above personality. This layer is strengths.

According to Gallup, only *1 in 33 million* people share the same top five strengths. You are unique, from the way you approach your job to how you perform in a role. Simple awareness of your strengths and how they influence your work is powerful. You can leverage this knowledge to seek projects in which you will excel, and pursue tasks and goals that come naturally to you.

According to Gallup, work that leverages one's natural talents positively impacts productivity, stress, and quality, resulting in a six-fold increase in employee engagement. If you know your strengths, you can target roles that use them fully. Your stress levels will decrease, just as your productivity and quality will rise.

Awareness of your natural talents equips you to be intentional in using them. When you play to your strengths, your work is energizing. Earlier, my mother referred to her *Strategic* strength:

> "I found it interesting that the executives would come and talk to me. Years later I realized they came to me because of my *Strategic* strength. That was the beginning of the realization I could coach people."

Strategic thinkers can pinpoint trends, notice problems, and identify opportunities many people overlook. This ability and way of thinking is why executives would come to her. Strategy is a buzzword these days, but many people are not strategic thinkers.

When executives talked to my mom, she recognized potential consequences and devised alternative suggestions and courses of action. This knack for identifying problems and generating alternative solutions gave her a voice with decision-makers.

How powerful would it be to know your strengths and to exercise them with intention, rather than occasionally tripping over success by chance?

Strengths, like personality, are something you are born with. But unlike disposition or temperament, strengths are in-born talents. With over 40 years of data, the Gallup Organization developed the Clifton StrengthsFinder assessment, which defines 34 natural talents in humans.

Think of the ability to think strategically, to generate ideas, to listen with empathy, to build rapport with strangers, and see potential in others.

Strengths are not limited to particular personality dispositions. Any of the personality styles we reviewed can have the natural ability to recognize potential in others, or the capacity to be analytical or strategic.

People often encounter two barriers to strengths identification:

Blind spots – Not recognizing or accepting they're better at something than most others.

Believing a strength isn't special – For instance, people who are expert at managing chaos and remaining productive when situations and environments are shifting may chalk it up to simply 'doing what you have to do' to keep things moving forward. They don't recognize this as a talent, and one that many people lack. In times of chaos, most people become unproductive or shut down. Not people with the *Arranger* strength; they thrive in chaos!

What Makes You Great?

What are you ridiculously good at? Knowing who you are and understanding what you do best is critical in every step of your career journey; from targeting career choices to having confident networking conversations. This awareness is important for resume and cover letter preparation, a top-notch interview performance and ultimately, performing at your best.

If you were asked what you do better than most people, what would you say? What makes you *great?* Are you pursuing positions that your strengths and abilities are best suited for?

Role mismatch is often cited as the number one reason for employee under-performance. Job fit matters! You don't want to regret accepting a position after one month on the job, and you certainly don't want to spend 10 years of your life in a career to realize it's a poor fit for your abilities and interests.

When you're seeking a new position, it's critical to articulate what you do best and how you can meet the needs of a customer or an employer. You are a walking advertisement. Is your ad convincing?

What about interviews?

Thanks to the groundwork laid by leadership and strength pioneers such as Peter Drucker and Donald Clifton, discovering and leveraging strengths is a common topic in corporate dialogue.

Imagine your next job interview. How would you answer the question "What are your strengths?"

Just for fun, take 30 – 60 seconds right now and try to articulate two or three of your strengths.

So what makes *you* great?

Would an employer have been impressed? Could you answer without hesitation? Could you confidently explain the value of these strengths?

If the answer to any of these questions is "no", you have some work to do, and identifying your unique strengths is the most important priority! Before you can uncover and share your strengths, you must learn what a strength is... and what it is not.

Imagine you are a hiring manager in an interview and you ask, "What are your greatest strengths?" How would you react to a candidate who told you their most impressive and differentiating strength – *the one thing they do best* – is professionalism? Commitment? Integrity?

Poised, committed, and a person of integrity are legitimate descriptions of character. They should not, however, be what you put forth as your greatest strengths.

Let me ask you another way: Would you hire someone whom you believed lacked integrity, commitment, or professionalism? Of course not! You must become aware of your natural talents to differentiate yourself and paint the most compelling, accurate picture of what makes you unique. Professionalism is not a differentiator; it is a "price of admission" requirement.

Not knowing who you are and what you do best is like wandering through life blindfolded, throwing darts, and hoping to hit the target. A lack of self-knowledge prevents intentional investment in your personal growth.

Having the language to articulate your strengths enables you to tell a compelling story, explaining what you do best is a match for what an employer needs most. When my clients see their strengths assessment results they almost always respond this way:

"I wish I knew this about myself years ago!"

"I recognize these things about myself, but I didn't have the words to explain it."

Knowing my personality tendencies, strengths, and workplace behaviors has been a game-changer for me. It gave me an advantage over other people: I landed every job I ever interviewed for, even when I didn't meet the job requirements. It was because I clearly described what I could do for the employer better than other candidates, using strengths-based results I had previously achieved.

Where do your strengths fall?
In addition to knowing *what* your strengths are, you can learn *where* your strengths fall, thematically. There are four themes, or categories, for the 34 strengths measured by the StrengthsFinder assessment:

Relating themes are ***outward*-**focused (external to you) and explain how people build connections with others. People with multiple *Relating* themes tend to enjoy working in teams, one-on-one, with others.

- Adaptability
- Connectedness
- Developer
- Empathy
- Harmony

- Inclusiveness
- Individualization
- Positivity
- Relator

Influencing themes are also ***outward***-focused and explain how people motivate others to action. People with multiple *Influencing* themes usually prefer a variety of different people to work with, and enjoy motivating and influencing people.

- Activator
- Command
- Communication
- Competition
- Maximizer
- Significance
- Self-Assurance
- Woo

Executing themes are ***inward***-focused (internal to you) and explain what drives people toward results. People with multiple strengths in the *Executing* theme are doers.

- Achiever
- Arranger
- Belief
- Consistency
- Deliberative
- Discipline
- Focus
- Responsibility
- Restorative

Thinking themes are also *inward*-focused and explain how people analyze the world. People with multiple strengths in the *Thinking* theme enjoy thinking more than doing.

- Analytical
- Context
- Futuristic
- Ideation
- Input
- Intellection
- Learner
- Strategic

Let's try something. Imagine some of your strengths are *Futuristic, Ideation, Analytical, and Empathy.*

The task at hand requires you to influence people, but like many people with multiple Thinking strengths, you have a tendency to live in your head and make decisions independently.

What can you do? In this instance, you could rely on your Empathy strength – seeing the world through others' eyes, and anticipating their needs – to compensate, ensuring a more collaborative approach.

Become intimately acquainted with your strengths. Read your results, underline or highlight the passages in your report that resonate with you, jot down examples of times you've used your strengths in different areas of your life, and create examples around the positive outcomes facilitated by these strengths.

As Socrates said, "Knowing thyself is the beginning of wisdom." There is tremendous value in knowing your natural talents, including the ability to answer behavioral-based interview questions with more substance, a more accurate assessment of your strengths, and why you're the right person for a promotion.

Familiarity with your strengths can also lead to more effective networking, or determining if you should start your own business, and where you might need support.

Some additional advantages of knowing your strengths are:

- Increased self-esteem
- A positive focus, away from negative self-talk and limiting beliefs
- A clear language to describe yourself, which is a valuable asset in cover letters, resumes, LinkedIn profiles, interviews, and networking conversations

I know my top five strengths. Now what?

A client told me that during a job interview, she was asked what words she would use to describe herself. How convenient! I had created a one-page summary of her strengths based on assessments she had done. She was able to provide a succinct summary of her strengths for them, like this:

- I'm committed, accountable, independent, trusted, and conscientious (*Responsibility*)
- I'm a problem solver, troubleshooter, and I find improvements and solutions (*Restorative*)
- I'm always learning and I catch on quickly (*Learner*)
- I grow talent in others, and enjoy helping others succeed (*Developer*)
- I'm a negotiator who sees both sides of a situation, enabling me to arrive at consensus (*Harmony*)

She was prepared to substantiate those strengths with behavioral examples, thanks to the reflection work she had done.

The employer was impressed with the way the interviewee had answered the question, and offered her the job. And guess what? My client declined the offer. She knew it wasn't the right role for her based on what she had learned about herself.

The true value of this assessment lies in effective interpretation of your results to make connections and provide insights you won't glean on your own. Too many people take this assessment, read their strengths, and then place the report in a drawer, never to be seen again. This is a missed opportunity!

I strongly recommend you seek out a coach who comes recommended by others for explaining StrengthsFinder effectively. After debriefing with your coach, practice explaining your strengths and discuss them with people who know you well to gain additional feedback.

Revealing the powerful narrative of your natural talents will serve you in so many ways in life.

One of my former clients had strengths in *Communication, Discipline,* and Winning Others Over *(WOO)*. When *WOO* and *Communication* are working together (these strength combinations are referred to as theme dynamics, or theme blends), she's the life of the party, networking, telling engaging stories, making friends, and building connections.

However, when *Discipline* (driven to create order and structure) and *Communication* lock arms, she is at home communicating policy, dictating standards, and ensuring people are compliant. One of those presentations of her personality is task-oriented (*Communication + Discipline*), while the other is relationship-oriented (*Communication + WOO*).

Understanding these tendencies increased this woman's understanding of her behavior and enhanced her awareness of how she may be perceived by co-workers, who may be confused by the shift between the different behaviors created by these strength combinations. This is a valuable insight.

Ask yourself:

1. How do my strengths influence my current, or a desired, role? Do I use my strengths daily?
2. What are some ways my strengths are unique in how I approach my work?
3. Am I able to identify potential gaps between strengths my job requires, and my strengths?
4. How might I leverage other strengths to bridge gaps?
5. Are my strengths revealing what I already suspected? Hint: "I need to make a change!"

Finally, take action:

- If employed, explain your strengths to your manager; help them find better ways to use your gifts!
- Be mindful of strengths when setting goals; you'll perform better.
- Look for special projects that need your strengths; it's a chance to shine.
- Keep strengths in mind when identifying your next career step.
- If job-seeking, embed strengths in your networking pitch, interview stories, cover letters, resume, and LinkedIn profile.
- Practice sharing your strengths; the more you practice, the more fluent you'll be.

Take StrengthsFinder
Cost: $15.00

https://www.gallupstrengthscenter.com/Purchase/en-US/ Product?Path=Clifton % 20StrengthsFinder

Character Strengths

Another interesting layer to strengths discovery are your character strengths. According to research available on *viacharacter. org*, a free online assessment, knowing and applying your unique character strength profile increases your life satisfaction and personal well-being.

Do you notice when there is something in the character of others that makes them stand out? Have you ever wondered what your character strengths are? Identifying these traits provides an additional lens to examine how and why you approach life the way you do.

The VIA Character report provides 20 character traits, ranked strongest to weakest, such as *Creativity, Perseverance, Curiosity, Social Intelligence,* and *Love of Learning.*

My top character strength is *Perspective,* which enables me to provide wise counsel to others. Perspective means having ways of looking at the world that make sense to oneself/others. As a coach, this is one more affirmation of why I'm wired for my work.

After you take this free assessment, think about how well your character strengths align with your life, the work you're doing now, as well as what you've done in the past.

If you'd like to discover your character strengths, the VIA Character Assessment is a great source of additional self-descriptors that are useful for reflection and personal branding. The assessment also offers additional data regarding potential role suitability.

Imagine you have *Love of Learning* as a top character strength, yet you work in a routine job that doesn't afford opportunities to learn and grow. This is a red flag.

VIA Character Strengths
Cost: Free

From the VIA Institute on Character:

"Research tells us that individuals who use their character strengths lead happier, more satisfying lives. Only when you understand your unique character strengths can you begin to live a life that is engaging, exciting and rewarding to YOU."

VIA Character Strengths Assessment
https://www.viacharacter.org/Survey/Account/Register

Competencies
A competency is an ability that contributes to successful outcomes in a particular role. The capacity to perform in a specific area is based on your **experience, skills, strengths, knowledge**, and **personality traits**. In other words, the layers of the Human Iceberg *combine* to create your competencies!

Let's look at an example competency:

Creativity: personally adds value to any task; is innovative, resourceful, inventive; can dream up new marketing and other business strategies.

Creativity is not a personality trait, nor a natural talent (i.e., strength). *Creativity* is not optimism, trust of others, nor a low need for planning. Yet, according to Paradigm Personality Labs (formerly the Center for Applied Cognitive Studies), creativity is defined as a combination of optimism, trust of others, imagination, spontaneity, comfort with complexity and change, and a lower need for organization, neatness, and methodicalness.

Your unique composition includes abilities (competencies) that are energizing or natural for you. Alternatively, your blend of traits influences your reaction to circumstances that drain you or are outside of your comfort zone.

When you think of moments you've been energized at work, you were using abilities that were *most* natural to you. Conversely, when you went home exhausted, you were engaging in activities that were *least* natural to you.

You can excel in a competency that isn't a natural talent. However, these competencies sap energy even though you perform well. Discover your energizing and natural competencies!

Competency Assessment: WorkPlace Big Five

The WorkPlace Big Five, created by Paradigm Personality Labs, is my favorite assessment. It reveals workplace behaviors, using a 5-factor personality model.

The assessment measures:

- How you respond to stressful situations
- Your tolerance of stimulation from people and your environment
- Your openness to new experiences, ideas, and change
- How easily, or to what degree of difficulty, you defer to others
- Your focus on work, goal accomplishment, and the need for achievement and success

These behaviors are building blocks to understand your work preferences, and determine how energizing, natural, or comfortable specific workplace activities are.

This table depicts the 54 competencies, grouped by category:

Interpersonal Skills	Leadership	Managing Others
Comfort with Diversity Facilitation Humor Informing others Listening Teamwork and cooperation	Ambition Basic leadership orientation Development of people Diplomacy Entrepreneurship Motivation of others Political savvy	Decision-making skills Delegation Follow through Hiring and staffing Meeting management Objectivity Performance focus
Self-Management		**Work Mechanics**
Action orientation Comfort working independently Reliability and consistency Responsibility acceptance Self-control Self-development Work/life balance	**Competencies** **by** **Theme Category**	Analytical thinking Business acumen Keyboarding accuracy Comfort with paperwork Numerical accuracy Technical learning Written communication
Managing Processes	**Sales**	**Professional Growth**
Adherence to policy Managing through systems Organization Planning Quality orientation Safety orientation Customer service orientation	Competitiveness Optimism Presentation skills Sales orientation Self-confidence	Comfort with ambiguity Comfort with innovation Creativity Flexibility Future thinking/visionary Overseas work success Range of perspectives/interests

I once had a client who was exhausted by managing people, even though she was disposed to taking charge in leadership situations. Yet her competencies revealed that most activities listed under the *Managing Others* theme were draining to her!

Identifying her competencies helped us discover career path options that do not require managing people, and fit her abilities and interests. We charted an ideal path for her as an individual contributor; targeting roles that employed her process improvement expertise and understanding of complex systems.

If you'd like to try an interesting exercise, download my free competency self-assessment! *http://www.virtuscareers.com/*

Documents/Follow % 20Your % 20Star/Competency % 20Self % 20 Assessment.docx

Contact me at *www.virtuscareers.com* to learn more about WorkPlace Big Five.

Work Focus

Work, at the fundamental level, can be reduced to four focuses:

1. Individuals with a *People* focus primarily enjoy working with others; leading, caring, supporting, serving, and selling.
2. Individuals with an *Ideas* focus primarily enjoy working with knowledge, theories, creativity, and insights.
3. Individuals with a *Things* focus primarily enjoy working with objects, e.g., machines, tools, animals, natural, and fabricated resources.
4. Individuals with a *Data* focus primarily enjoy working with numbers, facts, filing, procedures, and inspection.

Determining which of these areas appeals most to you is key to discovering the work for which you are wired. You may gravitate to one focus, however many people have a preference for two focus areas, or even an equal distribution across all four areas.

Determining Your Work Focus

Take a moment to review the example activities under each focus area (*Figure 1d*). Count the activities that appeal to you under each header.

Figure 1d

People	Data	Things	Ideas
Coach	Document	Repair	Write
Network	Summarize	Inventory	Strategize
Collaborate	Categorize	Test	Invent
Teach	Track	Transport	Present
Serve	Correlate	Maintain	Develop
Lead	Research	Purchase	Question
Resolve Conflict	Review	Package	Organize
Sell	Investigate	Operate	Explain
Coordinate	Edit	Troubleshoot	Problem Solve
Interview	Audit	Inspect	Innovate
Team Build	Calculate	Assemble	Market
Negotiate	Analyze	Collect	Communicate
Advise		Build	Forecast
Total:	Total:	Total:	Total:

Which work focus has the highest total? What is your second highest?

When you pair your strongest work focus with your second strongest work focus, interesting insights form. The secondary work focus preference can influence the primary preference considerably!

Imagine you have a primary interest in *Things* (e.g., repairing and troubleshooting) and a secondary interest in *Ideas* (e.g., inventing and developing), a more creative focus on *Things* would be fitting. You might find career satisfaction in a job like graphic design, developing creative digital content using computer software.

Alternatively, if your primary focus is *Things*, and *People* are your secondary area of focus, you might be better suited to a role like desk-side support, where you're working with computers and visiting employee workstations.

It's a good idea to do an interest inventory: list your hobbies, experiences, and the activities you enjoy and appreciate. For example, if you have a *people* and *things* focus and you enjoy baking, how might you combine those focus areas with your interest in baking?

Job Content

In addition to work focus, investigate job types that appeal to you. *Job types* are derived from Holland's Theory of Careers and Vocational choice, known as Holland Codes.

There are six job types associated with personality preference:

1. **Realistic** jobs are practical, physical, concrete, hands-on, machine, and tool-oriented. They often involve working with the hands or outdoors (e.g., firefighter, mechanic, contractor).
2. **Investigative** jobs solve puzzles, research, detect, or experiment. Jobs in this category are analytical, intellectual,

scientific, explorative, and thinking-oriented (e.g., police work, scientific research, lab technician).

3. **Artistic** jobs involve creativity, such as writing, photography, graphic artistry, architecture, and interior decorating. Jobs in the artistic category are creative, original, independent, inventive, and often involve media, graphics, and text.

4. **Social** jobs serve society in some way, e.g., teaching, social work, counseling, health care, or ministry. Social jobs are cooperative, supportive, with a focus on helping, healing, nurturing, and teaching.

5. **Enterprising** jobs involve making, selling, or managing products or services. They are often competitive environments that involve leadership, persuading, and status.

6. **Conventional** jobs involve working in an office such as management, financial transactions, and Information Technology. These jobs usually require detail-orientation and skill in organizing and administration.

Try this free Career test; it provides a list of 20 suggested occupations that fit your unique *Holland Code.*
https://www.123test.com/career-test/
After you complete the test, you can access the *ACT World of Work Map,* an online tool which displays job families based on work focus preference. This will provide ideas for roles that may appeal to you. The online interactive map graphically illustrates how occupations relate to each other based on work tasks.

Let's look at an example. Referencing *Figure 1e,* I selected the *Engineering & Technologies* job family, under the *Ideas* and *Things* work focus. This allows me to view related roles, with detailed information about each one.

Figure 1e

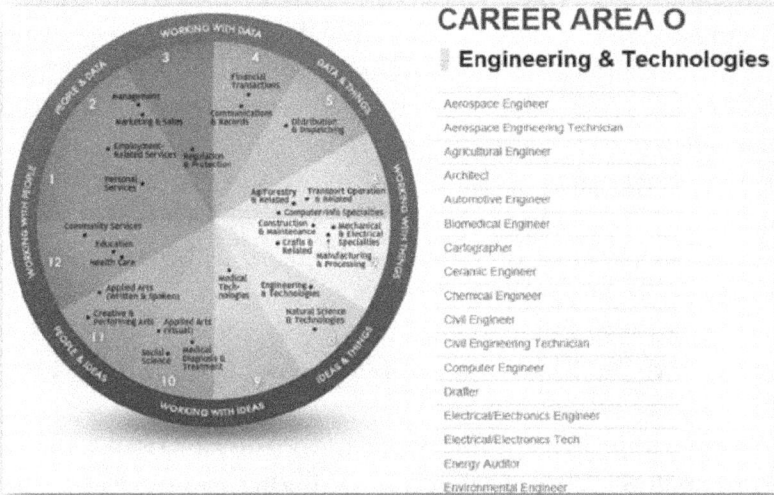

*Interactive ACT World of Work Map Online https://www.act.org/
content/dam/act/unsecured/multimedia/wwmap/world.html*

O*Net Online

*If you take the free Holland Code career test provided to obtain career
ideas, or generate ideas using the Work Focus exercise combined with the
World of Work Map, you can research roles using O*Net Online.* O*Net
is a free online tool for career exploration and job analysis. It is
for use by job seekers, workforce development and HR professionals, students, and researchers.

Once you identify career options of interest, O*Net (*www.
onetonline.org*) provides comprehensive and detailed role descriptions, including salary, education requirements, daily tasks,
competencies required, and Holland Code match. You can also
search job openings in your location, filtering by activities, skills,
abilities, interests, and values.

Feasibility/Desirability Matrix

Identifying possibilities can create hard decisions. To aid decision-making, I've created a Feasibility/Desirability Matrix, which you can download from the Additional Tools & Resources section (*Figure 1f*). This simple process helps you select a feasible option that has the highest desirability.

Using the matrix, list roles of interest in the *Role* column. Next, research each role using O*Net or a similar tool. Discover what kind of skills and education are required for each role; list these under the *Skills/Education Needed* column. You should also talk to people in those roles to find out how they spend their day, rather than make assumptions about how they spend it.

Next, rank the *feasibility* of each job. You can rank using numerical scales (1, 2, 3) or descriptors (high, medium, low). When assessing feasibility, consider resources at your disposal, such as finances and time; prerequisites; and ability to develop the skills and gain the education required.

Finally, rank the *desirability* of each job, based on your level of interest or passion. Be sure to reference the feature in O*Net that notes whether your choices are in growing or shrinking professions.

Figure 1f

Role	Skill/Education Needed	How Feasible	How Desirable
Role 1			
Role 2			

Past Experiences

Psychologist Tom Ward discovered that when people are faced with situations that require creativity, they tend to rely on past experience. For example, when study participants were asked to draw an alien, many people drew a familiar animal and modified it. Even when instructed to be "out-of-the-box creative", subjects rely on the familiar, resulting in drawings that possess traits of animals found on Earth, complete with symmetrical body parts, legs, eyes, and other common features.[4]

How does this relate to your career?

Relying on the familiar to determine options for the future inhibits you from even considering potential career opportunities. This is why others see beyond limitations you put on yourself – they have different experiences and perspectives.

To overcome behavior patterns and decisions that keep us stuck, we must gain an awareness of how restricted our thinking is.

How can you combat this limited viewpoint?

When you discuss your circumstances with people who think differently, they bring a fresh perspective, and influence you to think in a new way. As a caveat, keep in mind what I mentioned previously about advice from people who do not share your values!

If you reframe your situation and apply it to another person, would your recommendations and conclusions remain the same? That's something to think about!

The experiences you've had shape who you are. Your personal history, such as the location where you grew up, and the parenting style you were raised under, helps explain your triggers and viewpoints. It's important to recognize how past experiences shape present behavior, and become aware of the baggage we sometimes carry because of things that have happened in our lives.

Your experiences also yield insight to what you enjoyed or valued in the past. It's these experiences that help people know what they *don't* want in a career. Perhaps you tried customer service and found dealing with angry customers stressful. Maybe you did a stint in sales and struggled to meet your targets because you didn't like selling products people didn't need.

In my career, I was unsatisfied when I was micro-managed, blocked from doing projects I believed in, or assigned to tasks I didn't care about.

The first time I took WorkPlace Big Five, I noticed my high *Take Charge* and *Imagination* scores. Here was the reason I was so frustrated when the exciting ideas I generated were refused. I found that changing managers didn't help, because the problem was, I had a manager. The solution to my problem was to be my own boss. I wanted autonomy and control over my ideas and work. Reflecting on my career history, I now saw plainly that my third most important value – *Autonomy* – was the source of my career frustration.

Take the time to make a list of your experiences, including volunteer work, travel, and extra-curricular activities, and underline the experiences you valued and enjoyed. Ask yourself, what are the characteristics of those experiences that made them valuable to me? The answer to this question is a goldmine of information.

Personal Reflection

In addition to exploring each layer of the human iceberg, it is helpful to complete personal reflection exercises. I recommend using a dedicated journal or a notebook for this discovery process. I've included a list of questions to help you begin:

- Think of your best job. What made it the best? Remember to consider volunteer work and other experiences, as well as paid work.
- When have you felt energized at work? What were you doing?
- What do you love to do? E.g., spending time outdoors, developing meaningful relationships, working alone to analyze data, problem-solving, listening to people share their challenges.
- What experiences have you found valuable?
- What do you do better than most people? Ask others to answer this question.
- How would people who know you well describe you in three words?
- What activities do you enjoy?
- What activities do you *dislike?* What are things you want that you don't currently have?
- What do you *need* from your work? What are the deal-breakers (i.e., the essentials) that must be present in your work?

If you've been looking into the tools and techniques covered in this book, it should have cast some light onto your unique career discovery process.

Now let's look at a client case study.

Career Discovery Case Study

My client Samantha is a young mom of two. She recently decided to re-enter the workforce, and she was overwhelmed. She did not have a college degree, and she was unsure where to begin. I suggested she use the Human Iceberg model to discover her personality and strengths.

Let's take a look at her results:

Samantha's DiSC Profile:

Samantha's DiSC profile is *Influencing* and *Steady* (*IS*). The profile of an *IS* personality is:

- An approachable and understanding person.
- Optimistic, looks for the best in others.
- A good listener, offering constructive advice rather than imposing ideas and values on others.
- Develops and maintains relationships - at work and at play.

Samantha's Top 5 Strengths:

Belief – You have core values that are unchanging. Out of these values emerge a defined purpose for your life. Your friends describe you as dependable and easy to trust. Your work must mesh with your values.

Connectedness – You have faith in the links between all things. You believe there are few coincidences and that almost every event has a reason. You are a bridge builder among people who share differences.

Responsibility – You take psychological ownership of what you say you will do, feeling duty bound to follow it through to completion. This near obsession for doing things right and your impeccable ethics create your reputation as utterly dependable.

Restorative – You are adept at dealing with problems. You enjoy the challenge of analyzing symptoms, identifying what's wrong and finding the solution. It energizes you. You enjoy bringing things 'back to life.'

Woo – You love the challenge of meeting new people and 'winning others over.' You enjoy breaking the ice and making a connection with another person. In your world there are no strangers, just friends you haven't met yet.

Samantha's results revealed she is best suited for a *people-focused* job. Her primary and secondary DiSC styles are relationship-oriented; her strength themes are heavily represented in *Relating* and *Influencing* themes, both of which are outward-facing.

Work Focus
Samantha then completed the *Work Focus* exercise. She checked off desirable activities under the *People, Things, Ideas,* and *Data focus areas.* A tally of her selections identified her focus areas as *People* and *Data.*

Samantha's Job Family Matches
A job family is defined as a series of related jobs distinguished by levels of knowledge, skills, and abilities (competencies) and other factors.

Samantha used the *World of Work Map* to identify job families, or career clusters, that were categorized under the *People* and *Data* work focus.

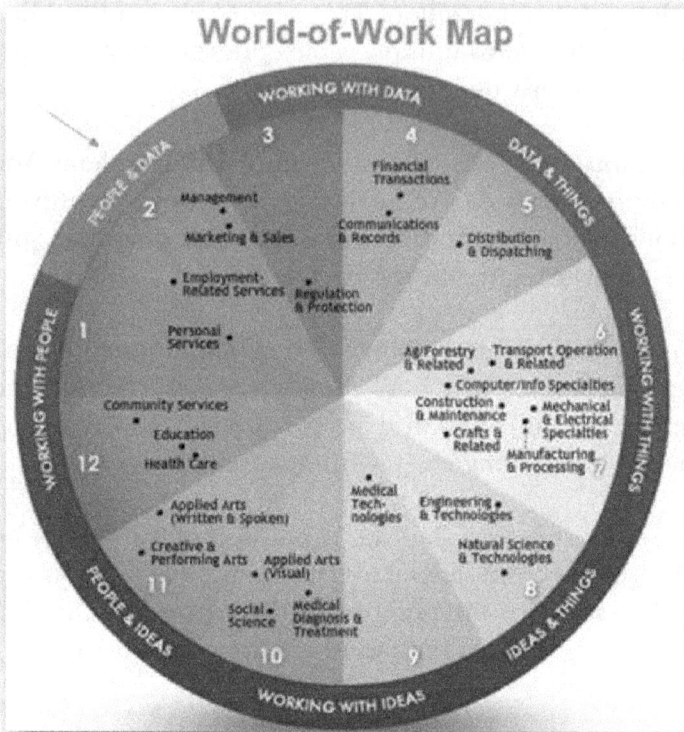

Samantha's job family matches are:

1. **Management**: executive, executive secretary, purchaser, general manager, property manager, financial manager, office (medical/legal/etc.) manager, retail store manager, hotel/motel manager, food service manager
2. **Marketing & Sales**: insurance agent, real estate agent, travel agent, buyer, sales representative, manufacturer's representative, retail sales worker, telemarketer, route driver, stock broker, counter sales (e.g., auto/medical/etc. supplies)
3. **Employment-Related Services**: human resources jobs, including both management positions and specialty jobs

as trainer, employee benefits specialist, salary administration, recruiter, interviewer, job analyst, coach, and
consultant

Samantha considered each job family and researched opportunities to learn more about the roles in each to decide what
interested her most. Her personality, strengths, values, work focus preferences, and competencies collected from the self-assessment exercises provided a wealth of data to guide her choices.
She reflected upon the transferrable skills she had acquired from
previous experience.

We reviewed the insights she had gained against each role
to decide which options best matched her profile, and how her
strengths would contribute to her performance in the role.

In Samantha's situation, the most desirable and feasible job
was a **Realtor**. She could attend a two-month training program
and obtain a state realtor license in a short period of time with a
modest financial investment.

Role	Skill/Education Needed	How Feasible	How Desirable
Recruiter	Bachelor Degree	Medium	Medium
Realtor	2 Mo. Course State License	High	High

When I first met Samantha she felt lost, discouraged, and
lacked hope. After taking these discovery steps, Samantha en-
rolled in Real Estate school and passed the licensing exam. She
is excited about her career, and is confident that she made a
well-informed choice.

Why did I spend so much time on finding your star before
introducing the five career success factors? Because you have a
decision to make: are you in the right career?

If you apply the success strategies to a career that's not a good fit, you're taking a bath in a muddy puddle. When you find work that you love and excel in, applying the success strategies will move you from mediocrity to mastery!

However, you may have concluded a career change is in order. If so, we have one more stop to make: Career Transition!

Career Transition

If you are considering a career change, you're not alone! A *Huffington Post* poll revealed almost 80% of workers in their 20s want to change careers, followed by 64% of those in their 30s, and 54% of workers in their 40s. Also, *73%* of these workers had not landed the job they expected.

The mental struggle that precedes a career change can be harder than actually making the change. I'm not going to tell you to drop everything and jump ship. Instead, I'd like to offer some important points to consider.

Ending up in a job you didn't expect isn't always a bad thing. However, Forbes reports only 19% of people surveyed by Right Management in the U.S. and Canada said they were satisfied with their jobs, while 16% said they were somewhat satisfied. The rest, a whopping 65%, said they were unhappy at work.

Here are some important considerations when making career change decisions:

Weigh the Advice of Others

The advice of your friends, family, and co-workers can make you feel stuck in your current situation, so it's important to recognize that people come to the table with their own bias, even if it's at a subconscious level.

- *Co-workers have a vested interest in your decision.* They have something to lose if you leave, e.g., loss of camaraderie, increased workload, or envy because they can't leave.
- *Family members have a vested interest in your decision.* The self-preservation instinct may kick in if you're considering a path that's unproven, or carries some risk if they rely on you for support. Even supportive people are

susceptible to reactions of self-preservation if their safety and security feel threatened.

- **People who know you best may struggle to see you in a different context.** If you're an accountant, but wish to become a self-employed children's entertainer, your accountant identity is deeply seeded in the minds of those closest to you. Because of the strong association, those people may have difficulty seeing you in a new context. There's value in the opinions of others, but if the instinct to try something new is strong, don't ignore it. Don't brush aside your dreams because others don't see your vision.

Many people react negatively to change, but it doesn't mean you're making a poor choice. Valid and reliable assessments are one way to confirm those instincts, as well as talking to people in the line of work you are interested in.

To be clear, I'm not suggesting you disregard the concerns of your loved ones about your prospective career change. People often present objections without stating their core concern. The good news is, once you identify the root cause of their fears, you can create a plan that everyone can support.

There are, however, two questions that you can use to uncover the root cause of their objections.

My husband was concerned when I wanted to quit my job to open my own business. To move beyond surface-level objections, I asked the following questions:

- What is the greatest concern you have about this change?
- What would it take for that threat to be removed?

My husband was concerned we wouldn't be able to meet our financial obligations if I could no longer count on a steady paycheck. He indicated he would feel more comfortable with the change if I saved enough to cover six months' expenses, and that I would return to corporate work if I wasn't able to make ends meet with my business.

Voilà! These agreements allayed his concerns and he was fully supportive of my plans to launch my own business.

Be aware of your own blind spots

Herminia Ibarra, a Professor of Organizational Behavior at INSEAD, has done extensive research on career changers. What she discovered is that people can tell you exactly what they *don't want* to do and why, but they usually can't tell you what they want to do *instead.* I've observed this in my clients, as well.

Ibarra's research suggests the way we think about what we're good at is limiting and tends to be functionally specific; or, tied to what we've historically done. Instead, think of your skills as *portable competencies* that can be applied in a wider range of contexts.[5]

Figuring out what you *don't* want is as valuable as knowing what you *do* want. My grandmother used to say identifying a problem is 80% of the way to a solution.

If you feel discouraged because the vision isn't clear, try revisiting the *Find Your Star* section and working through the career discovery tools. The first step of career change is recognizing your unique gifts and abilities, and how your experiences can transfer to new opportunities.

For example, early in my career I worked in IT as a lead software developer. While the core tasks of my job were very technical, I developed many transferable skills, such as:

- Onboarding and training new team members
- Training processes and documentation
- Presentation skills
- Delegation

- Project life-cycle
- Project estimation
- Multi-project management
- Effective communication skills
- Negotiation tactics
- Advanced Excel skills
- Trend analysis and analytical thinking skills
- S.WO.T. analysis
- Working on cross-functional teams
- Contractor/vendor relationship management
- Meeting management
- Process and quality improvement
- Ramping up on new projects in a short period of time

When you read this list, it doesn't come across as a technical job description.

Research by Korn Ferry International suggests **15% of skills are specific to a job, while 85% of skills are more general and transferable across roles**. Think about your experience in terms of portable competencies, and how you might apply them in new ways.

For instance, there are key skills most employers desire:

- Meeting deadlines
- Problem-solving
- Organizing and managing projects
- Managing people
- Negotiation skills
- Computer skills
- Public speaking
- Effective writing
- Managing budgets
- Customer focus

In addition to those coveted skills, there are common categories most skills fall within, such as:

- *Working with things:* assembling, operating tools, repairing, driving/operating vehicles
- *Dealing with data:* analyzing, investigating, auditing, budgeting, recording, calculating, classifying, inspecting, evaluating, counting, research, detail orientation, compiling, synthesizing
- *Working with people:* instructing, demonstrating, helping, counseling, listening, persuading, supervising, coaching, understanding, interviewing, being patient, giving insight, diplomacy
- *Working with words and ideas:* public speaking, writing clearly, designing, inventing, editing
- *Leadership skills:* motivating, having self-confidence, negotiation, decision-making, planning, delegating, directing, explaining, getting results, solving problems, taking risks, mediating problems, running meetings, being competitive
- *Artistic/Creative skills:* drawing, self-expression, presenting, performing, dancing, playing instruments

Rather than focus on experience you don't have, identify the skill categories and themes the employer is looking for.

Imagine the role you are interested in requires working with people and data. List the relevant skills you have, including concrete examples and stories. Quantify your examples whenever possible, including the outcome. Tie this narrative back to the new opportunity to make the connection clear to an employer.

One of my recent clients transitioned from a Technical Writer role to a Business Analyst, with no prior direct experience. We clearly outlined how her experience and skills translated to the requirements of the new role. She performed strongly during the interview process and received a job offer. You may be pleasantly surprised you have more to offer than you first thought. Take time to inventory your transferrable skills!

Recognize there's risk in staying

Change can be difficult and scary. A sound decision begins with confidence in who you are and what you offer, discerning good advice from bad, and working to gain alignment with loved ones to support your career choices.

If you're staying in a role that's sucking the joy out of you, you should consider the costs of staying. For instance, there is the opportunity cost of not learning new skills, a lack of fulfillment, increased stress, poor health, negative effect on your family, decreased productivity, poor performance, low quality of work, a negative attitude, and lack of motivation.

Are you ready to learn about the five success strategies? Let's get to it!

PART 3

The Five Success Strategies

Where do the five success strategies come from? Why these five?

Valerie McMurray, creator of the WISE Profile, set out to discover critical factors for career and leadership success in women for her graduate thesis. She conducted a research study and interviewed successful female CEOs, and senior leaders one level below CEO, as well as subject matter experts in women's leadership. She also conducted an extensive review of the literature on the subject.

Through her extensive analysis, five success factors became clear to McMurray. She explains:

"Once these five factors were identified, a second research study was conducted to define these factors and develop, administer, and validate an assessment that would measure the five factors for career and leadership success. On the surface these seem to be very broad factors, but closer examination revealed that these five success factors had specific definitions.

An extensive coding process was conducted to gain the meaning of these five factors as described by the women interviewed, the subject matter experts, and the literature on the factors. It became clear that a specific defined meaning of these five factors contribute to a woman's career and leadership success. These factors were foundational to success and even more importantly, each one built on the others."

Each of the success factors contributed to my mom's success. Let's look at them in more detail.

Success Strategy #1: Self-Awareness/Openness to Feedback

The Top Predictor of Career Success

Green Peak Partners, an organizational consulting firm, commissioned a study called, *"What Predicts Executive Success?"*[6] The study was conducted by a team of researchers at Cornell University's School of Industrial and Labor Relations. They investigated leadership styles, backgrounds, and performance of 72 executives representing 31 companies. Half of the executives had a C-level or President-level role at public and private equity firms.

The researchers discovered that tough, results-at-all-costs executives actually *weaken* the bottom line, while self-aware leaders with strong interpersonal skills deliver better financial results.

Overall, a high self-awareness score is the strongest predictor of success. "Executives who are aware of their weaknesses are often better able to hire subordinates who perform well in areas in which the leader lacks acumen," said Dr. Becky Winkler, Principal at Green Peak.

McMurray defines Self-Awareness/Openness to Feedback as: "Seeking out opinions of others, candid feedback and self-learning for introspection leading to conscious knowledge and understanding of one's own behaviors, feelings, motives, character, values and goals. Working on areas that need improvement through reflection and understanding."

Let's look at some factors of self-awareness. As we do, ask yourself how self-aware you are?

The Need to be Right

In my younger years, being right was important to me. I often engaged in debate, staunchly defending my point of view. Yes, I have admittedly debated about the correct way to put toilet paper on the holder: flap in front, or flap in back. My high school principal told me I'd make an excellent lawyer. At the time, his comment fueled my pride. As an adult, I recognize it as a left-handed compliment.

I could not accept being wrong. A defining moment came when I called my mother to vent about a disagreement I'd had with a family member. She quietly listened as I presented my position. She would *surely* see things my way and accept that the other person was out of line.

When I was finished, she responded to me with a question: "How does being right serve you in life?"

I was speechless. "What do you mean?" I managed to reply.

My mom explained if being right was so important, it must serve a purpose. She was asking what that purpose was. My brain sifted through the ways being right had served me in life. What surfaced was not noble or pretty. *It proved I was smarter than the other person.*

I wasn't ready to admit this, so I remained silent. My mother asked, "How will it serve you well to always be right, but alienate everyone around you? Do you want to be right, or do you want to be happy?"

The words struck me so forcibly that even today, the question stays with me. It reshaped my thinking. My father once said it takes a person a lifetime to develop their opinion, and you're not going to change it in a single conversation. My mentor Steve Lishansky always says, "Being right is insufficient for being effective."

You know what I found out about the great toilet paper debate? When you want the paper to slide off the roll faster, flap in front works best. If you have toddlers, flap in back makes it harder to unroll all over the floor as quickly. I guess there's no right way to put toilet paper on the roll – only preference. Many things people argue about are not easily allocated to the right or wrong column.

7 lessons I've learned about being right:

1. My right is not someone else's right; they have a different perspective I know nothing about
2. Sometimes "right" is really just a preference
3. Relationships are more important than being right
4. The desire to be right blocks personal learning and happiness
5. The quest to be right keeps you in the weeds; you won't grow as a person if you can't see the big picture
6. Accepting that you don't need to be right deepens your maturity, builds a better reputation, and earns more respect than insisting on being right
7. Life holds less conflict when being right is no longer a priority

The dark, ugly world of Internet comment boards is fueled by the human need to be right. The next time you're tempted to prove you're right, consider what's motivating you. Is there a better choice to attract peace and happiness into your life?

Emotional Intelligence

Emotional intelligence (EI) or Emotional Quotient (EQ) is the capacity of individuals to recognize their own – and other people's – emotions, to discriminate between feelings and label them appropriately, and to use emotional information to guide thinking and behavior.[7]

Whether you're at the grocery store, in a job interview, at a networking event, or in a meeting, your level of EI leaves an impression on people every day. What impressions are you leaving? Your reputation doesn't reside in your mind, but in the minds of others. You must decide how you want to deal with this simple fact.

Self-awareness is the first step to increasing your EI. I want to share a simple process to begin a shift in the right direction, which involves requesting and reflecting upon feedback. I'll warn you upfront, you must be brutally honest with yourself, and prepare to accept some uncomfortable feedback. If accepting feedback is a challenge for you, I recommend you review the *Openness to Feedback* section later in this chapter before you try this exercise.

I. Solicit feedback from others
Asking questions of people with whom you have different relationships (e.g., co-workers, family, friends) can uncover valuable information.

Example questions:

- How do I tend to respond to conflict?
- What are 3 positive words or phrases you would use to describe me?
- What are 3 not-so-positive words or phrases you would use to describe me?
- What values and character strengths do I possess?
- What's your favorite thing about me?
- What's your least favorite thing about me?
- What personal improvements would you suggest I make?

It's important to reinforce the importance of honest answers. You want real feedback; not what others think you'd prefer to hear. When you do receive feedback, don't allow yourself to become defensive. Just listen and thank the other person. Discomfort always accompanies growth, so be gracious to people who care enough to tell you the good, the bad, and the ugly.

II. Reflect on your current cognitive stage

Psychologist Robert Kegan developed a theory of human development which outlines five cognitive levels, or stages. This abbreviated explanation of his model by Jay Barbuto, Director for The Center for Leadership at CSU Fullerton, will aid in self-reflection, and allow you to incorporate the feedback you received to help you objectively determine your current stage.

1st Level

Impulsive – A person is not able to think about what they're doing, just what their instincts cause them to do. This stage does not occur with adults, so I will not expand on it.

2nd Level

Imperial – This stage is about cause and effect. We are unable to separate ourselves from what we want and what we need to do to get it. We are able to control our impulses at this stage because we understand consequences. *People and relationships are viewed in terms of what we want from the situation or relationship.*

3rd Level

Interpersonalism – In this stage, we're able to think about what we want, and we're able to hold it separate from ourselves. What drives our thinking are inferences and generalizations, ideals, and values. *We get our identity and our belief system from some form of external reference;* our parents, what we learned in school, what the experts say, the authoritative opinions of others.

4ᵗʰ Level

Intrapersonal – At this stage, we can define who we are without being defined by others, while still considering what others say. This stage is about identity, autonomy, and individualization. We are consumed by who we are, and the kind of person we are. *We can't separate our identity or our own viewpoints from a situation.*

5ᵗʰ Level

Post-Modern – Most adults never reach 5ᵗʰ level cognition. It is at this stage that we hold our identity as object to us. We no longer think, "This is who I am and that's all there is to it." We are able to see nuances and complexities and *we realize the need to expand who we are and become open to other possibilities.* We are willing to reinvent our identity because we understand our identity is limited, and as circumstances continuously change we need to change with them.

5ᵗʰ Level is where:

- We listen more and speak less
- We offer grace, instead of criticism
- We allow others the spotlight
- We develop a thick skin
- We want the best for others
- We become curious about other perspectives

You may move between two stages, but where do you reside most often?

Watch Robert Kegan's Theory of Adult Development explained by Jay Barbuto: *https://www.youtube.com/watch?v=xUOapqI3rzs*

III. Monitor your thoughts

> "Change your thoughts and
> you change your world."
> - NORMAN VINCENT PEALE

Research shows that over time thoughts become beliefs and deeply held convictions because *80%* of our thoughts repeat themselves daily. The good news is, if you play positive tracks in your mind, you'll begin to believe them!

Adam Sicinski, creator of IQ Matrix and visual thinking expert, explains two laws at work[8]:

1. *Law of Concentration,* which states that what you think, emotionalize, and visualize continuously grows in your life
2. *Law of Becoming,* which states that you *attract* into your life the weaknesses, strengths, limitations, and abilities you have chosen to dwell upon most often

In a nutshell, thoughts become things.

Consciously examine the mental audio track you're playing every day for a whole week. How does your track sound?

"My situation is temporary. When I fail, I will accept defeat as temporary, learn from it, and won't take it as personal failure. Worry and self-pity are self-defeating. I believe I am destined for good things and will have everything I need."

"My situation is hopeless. I've tried everything and I'm not getting anywhere. I'm a failure. There are so many people out there who are successful. I just don't have what it takes, and I'll never go anywhere. This is never going to turn out. I guess I'm just destined to be a loser."

Dismiss negative thoughts and create a new track. Make that positive track a daily habit. As my pastor says, "The scene of the crime is your mind."

Admit when you need help
Take a critical look at your situation and identify what's not working with what you've been doing. You know the old saying: *Keep doing what you're doing, and you'll keep getting what you're getting.*

Identify two or three specific actions to move in the right direction to reach your goals. Think about the help you need and potential sources of help:

- Seek advice from others who've been in your circumstance: what suggestions might they offer?
- Consult with experts or professionals.
- Ask about and search online for non-profit and community resources at your disposal.

Regardless of how independent a person is, few reach the proverbial mountaintop without the helping hand of another, or more realistically, many helping hands.

Openness to Feedback

Being open to feedback is a foundation for self-awareness, and continuous growth and improvement. If you aren't aware of how you're perceived, or aren't open to hearing it, you may be puzzled by doors that slam in your face.

Recall this quote when my mom discussed receiving feedback from her boss, "I listened, and I learned." To the good news *and* the bad.

If you become defensive or make excuses when people try to give you constructive feedback, eventually they'll give up trying to talk to you. Before you wish them good riddance, remember that everyone is expendable. There is a cost to turnover and you don't want to be identified as the cause of it.

Few of us enjoy hearing about our shortcomings. It's human nature to preserve and protect ourselves by minimizing or rejecting negative characterizations from others.

Some people do genuinely solicit feedback, because they've experienced value from being open to the perspective of others, but that isn't the norm. That's why I've put together some tips to help you receive feedback more effectively:

Prepare

- Ensure it's a good time to receive feedback. If someone wants to speak with you and you are distracted or upset, schedule a time when you are more likely to be receptive. Explain you need time to focus so you can be present for the conversation.
- Consider your potential reactions to negative feedback. What might prevent you from being open? How might you avoid reacting defensively? One option is to consider the positive intentions the other person has in raising the issue. Give

their motives the benefit of the doubt, such as wanting the best for you and seeking to help you grow.

Stay open

- Respond in a way that demonstrates your willingness to see another person's point of view.
- Think about this: if the feedback were about someone else, would you be more likely to see its validity?
- Remind yourself that if this person made this observation, it's reasonable to think others have as well. Perception is reality, so how will you deal with the perceptions others have of you?

Use EI to respond thoughtfully

- Take a slow, deep breath before you respond to anything.
- Consider your tone and volume when you speak.
- Avoid accusations or defensiveness, e.g., "It's not my fault."

Consider what you might learn from the feedback

- Ask yourself what opportunity may exist for you to learn and grow as a person.

Work together to develop a plan

- Ask the person giving you feedback for their suggestions for how you might improve.

- Grant them permission to hold you accountable for any agreements you make.
- If you want support from the person to make progress toward change, ask if they are open to discuss ways they can support your improvement.

Tools to Build Self-Awareness
Competency Development
George Washington University – Learn Now: *https://ode.hr.gwu.edu/learn-now*
Emotional Intelligence Assessment (Free)
http://www.ihhp.com/free-eq-quiz/

Success Strategy # 2: Effective Communication Skills

Having an Executive Coach as your mother is an interesting experience. When I would go to my mom with a problem she would not advise me about what I should do about the problem. Rather, she coached me how to find a way to solve my problem.

She would listen intently and when I was done explaining, she would pause and say, "Okay..." Then she would ask a question. Rather than hand an answer to me, she communicated in a way that enhanced my critical thinking skills.

My mom has an uncanny ability to remain rational and calm, regardless of the subject. She always listens before she speaks. She asks questions and coaches you to see things from other perspectives, and does it in the most disarming way possible. That gives you space to realize that maybe you were the one who was wrong.

McMurray's WISE Profile defines *Effective Communication Skills* as "a range of behaviors and abilities used to express oneself and communicate effectively with others in a professional and personable manner. The art of persuasion using oral and written language that enables a woman to convey information, expectations and goals so that it is received and understood."

Let's look at practical ways to build communication skills.

One reason my mom is an effective, well-liked coach is that she is a good listener. Many people are *not* good listeners, for lots of reasons. They may prefer to talk, lack interest, or not want to invest the time or effort listening requires. Regardless of the reason, when you can't listen to what others have to say, you're sending a clear message that you don't value what that person has to say. Ouch!

Effective communication skills are prerequisite to strong relationships. Thus, poor listening leads to poor relationships.

Three Levels of Listening

Did you know there are two additional levels of listening? Practicing and using the three levels of listening will dramatically increase your communication skills.

Listening is more natural for some than others, but not as hard as you might think. The key is to:

1. Frame your thinking based on the *goal* of communication
2. Develop awareness and knowledge about the 3 levels of listening

Most think of communication as a means to convey and receive information, and that's not entirely correct. The goals of communication also include to *understand* and *to be understood.*

Most of us prioritize being understood yet when we prioritize understanding others, the second is more likely to be achieved. When you seek to understand others, they will respond by seeking to understand you in return. It's a beautiful reciprocity that you've influenced by leading with listening.

Let's approach listening from the context of seeking to understand:

Level 1: Listening for information

Most people don't move beyond this level. They listen long enough to grasp the basic message, then move into problem solving, defending, or some response to what has been said. The primary issue with this approach is there is much more to communication than what has been said.

Professor Albert Mehrabian and colleagues at UCLA found only 7% of communication is verbal, 55% is body language, and 38% is tone.

Level 2: Listening for impact

I went to the park with my daughter one morning and struck up a conversation with a young mother who asked what I did for a living. I told her I'm a Career and Executive Coach. She said, "Maybe you could help me. I still haven't figured out what I want to do when I grow up."

The young woman shared that she wasn't sure what she wanted to do: she didn't have a college degree, and she felt her options were limited.

I could have given her information on the mechanics of a job search and places that hire people without a college degree. Instead, I thought to myself, "What effect must this situation be having on this woman? She's feeling very uncertain. She hadn't planned to go back to work until her children were in school full-time. What are the fears and challenges this must be causing?"

Because I was listening for impact, I asked more questions and listened to her concerns and fears. This helped me understand her primary and most pressing need was not job search mechanics, it was support and confirmation that she had something of value to contribute to the world.

If you listen only for information, you are likely to forget something key: *the expressed need is often not the true need.*

We began to talk about strengths she possesses that someone would be willing to pay for, such as the natural ability to organize, or listening empathically to people.

She said she had not considered how her natural talents qualify her to make a contribution. Don't we all tend to fall into that trap from time to time? My mentor says it's like a bird lamenting they can't fly without having to use their wings.

Level 3: Listening for what's not being said

As I listened to the woman in the park speak of her career struggles, it enabled me to read what wasn't said directly: *She and her husband were not on the same page about her returning to work, and it was creating conflict.*

By adopting the three levels of listening, I determined how I might best help her, and the first step was most certainly *not* brushing up her resume. It was to help rebuild her confidence, and coaching her to have constructive dialogue with her husband to create alignment.

When your goal is to understand, you are in a position to meet the true need of the other person, whether it's a co-worker, your boss, or a stranger at the park.

Use Questions to Achieve Better Outcomes

The skill of using questions to influence positive outcomes is one of the best investments you can make, and it's valuable across countless situations. The best way to illustrate this power is with examples.

While I was having lunch with Jill, she shared the difficulty she was having with a business leader she interacted with regularly. This leader often complained and criticized Jill's boss, which was very uncomfortable for her; she did not agree with the criticism but she remained quiet. She was certain that directly addressing the comments would be uncomfortable and ineffective, if not counterproductive.

Also, stating how she was feeling put her in a position of having the legitimacy of her feelings judged by the other person. In a case like this, I advised Jill to use questions to influence a change in his behavior. That put the onus on the other leader to defend his behavior, rather than Jill being put over a barrel to defend her reaction to it. Two important notes before looking at examples:

- Questions must be asked in a neutral tone, free of sarcasm.
- Questions should not be presented as rhetorical.

If another party is gossiping or complaining to you, you might ask, "How would you like me to act on this information?" This tactfully demonstrates your wish to be included only in conversations when your involvement is appropriate or necessary.

Suppose the response is something like, "I'm just venting." In that case, you could ask a follow-up question, "Have you thought about providing feedback directly to Jane to allow her to address your concerns?"

This response is solution-focused and tactfully reinforces your unwillingness to participate in unproductive venting sessions.

This approach is also useful when you receive feedback that is inaccurate, unjust, or something that cannot be acted upon.

Laura was receiving unfair feedback from her manager because they had a personality clash. Her manager seemed interested in managing Laura out of the company. However, Laura was a top performer with an impeccable work record.

The only recourse her manager had to create a negative perception of Laura's performance was to offer vague, subjective criticism. This approach to providing feedback is used often, but it is neither constructive nor helpful because it can't be acted upon by the recipient.

In a recent performance review, Laura's manager couldn't find anything wrong with her core performance, but said she wasn't "communicating with corporate enough." Laura had work relationships in the field, and she knew there wasn't a reason for her to be communicating with corporate. She wasn't even sure who "corporate" referred to.

Regardless, it was documented in her performance review, and if she didn't meet her manager's unclear expectation of increased communication with the corporate office she was sure to get dinged on her next performance review.

If you are in a situation in which you are seemingly set up for failure, questions are a great strategy. In Laura's situation, I suggested she directly address the criticism by saying something like, "I'd be happy to communicate more with the corporate office. Which individuals should be included, what method and frequency of communication would you like me to use, and what key messages should be communicated?"

The key is to get the person to be specific. If Laura's manager can't answer these questions and define her expectations, she may be forced to admit more communication to corporate from Laura is not a true need.

Another tactic Laura could employ would be to say, "Thank you for telling me this; I've never heard this feedback before. How would you like me to act on it? What should I do differently, better, or more of, in the future?" Do you see how it forces the other person to provide clarity and specificity?

When faced with difficult people and unjust treatment, our inclination is to suffer in silence or create a defense. Putting yourself on the defense creates powerlessness and subordinates you to the other person.

In contrast, asking clarifying, well-positioned questions put you in control of the conversation and requires the other person to explain their stance and recognize implications they may not have considered.

The next time you're tempted to approach a situation with a defensive communication strategy, consider formulating constructive questions to re-frame the conversation instead. You'll gain more respect and have a more productive conversation.

Having Difficult Conversations

I've coached hundreds of people to prepare them for difficult conversations, and one commonality I find is the intense difficulty many people have approaching a co-worker or manager with constructive feedback.

Many people I've talked to would rather choose to find a new job than attempt to influence change in a difficult relationship. You know the saying, "People quit their boss, not their job."

Why do people avoid giving feedback? Here are some arguments – and counter arguments – I often hear:

"I tried before. It didn't make a difference."
Perhaps the method was ineffective. Are you open to a better approach?

"My boss is intimidating. I'm afraid to confront him/her."
What happens when you encounter an intimidating boss or co-worker at your next job? Wouldn't you like to learn to manage people once and for all? Avoid placing yourself in a subordinate, parent/child relationship with another person. It's not healthy.

"They might retaliate against me." or *"I'll get fired."*
If it's a bad situation, they're probably doing you a favor. No one exerts as much effort to find a job as someone who needs one. Also, this is why it's important to have three months of expenses saved if you're married, and six months of expenses saved if single. You don't have to be a slave to anyone.

"I don't want to hurt their feelings."
How would you feel if someone was upset about something you did? Would you prefer they resent you silently, or would you appreciate a chance to address the issue? Approach is everything. It's very simple to provide feedback in a non-threatening way. If you're hurting

someone, you're handling it incorrectly. Giving someone feedback shows you care enough about the relationship to speak up.

"I'm afraid it will damage our relationship."
Healthy conflict that is resolved is actually shown to strengthen and deepen relationships, not damage them. Again, approach is everything.

"I don't want to cause a problem."
Houston, we (already) have a problem.

What if they reject my feedback?
Giving feedback is hard for most people. And it's frustrating to have your feedback met with resistance, hostility, or rejection.

I'm going to share a marvelously simple way to bolster your courage to speak up. You can do a lot to make it easier for someone to respond favorably to feedback, through preparation and delivery.

Step 1: Before you say a word, reflect on these points:

- *Have I made my expectations clear?* When my oldest son reached a certain age we had different expectations around level of freedom once he had his own car. One weekend when our expectations didn't align, I realized I hadn't set my expectations up front, nor did I understand his. A simple conversation resolved our expectations and it was smooth sailing going forward.

- *Are my expectations realistic?* Ask at least two trusted, reasonable people, preferably with personalities different from your own, for alternate perspectives.
- *Am I being too sensitive?* Give yourself a cooling off period to consider other viewpoints. People say and do offensive things, but create a space between what happens to you, and your reaction. You have a choice in your reaction. I believe the world would be a much better place if we had thicker skins.
- *What is my motive?* Why are you giving feedback? Is it out of genuine care and concern for the relationship, or with the other person's best interest in mind? Be honest with yourself. What does your head say? What does your heart say? If your head and heart are aligned on a pure motive, you can proceed with confidence.
- *Am I making assumptions?* Things aren't always as they seem. I recall many times I made assumptions and was proven wrong. The late, great Dale Carnegie wisely compels us to *assume the nobler motive* in others. To guard against assumptions, become curious. Ask questions in a neutral tone: "I think I might be interpreting what you said in a way you didn't intend. Can we talk so I can better understand?"
- *Is this an appropriate time/place/medium for feedback?* Feedback should be given privately, at a fitting time, in person. Use the phone, if face-to-face is not possible. Feedback given before someone is about to deliver an important presentation, or when fighting a fire for a customer is ill-planned. Feedback should *not* be given in email or text messages. It may be misunderstood, and things will go sideways in a New York minute.

Step 2: Now, let's get to the nitty-gritty of giving feedback using three letters: **SBI**.

The Center for Creative Leadership developed the Situation Behavior Impact feedback model to help managers deliver clear, specific feedback; however, it works across all relationships, personal and professional.

First, describe the *when* and *where* of the **situation**.

Next, describe the other person's **behavior**, only mentioning actions you have *observed*. It is critical to remove assumptions of motive or intent, which almost always escalates conflict.

Next, communicate the **impact** of his or her behavior on you. When appropriate, discuss what you would like to see change in the future.

Before I give you an example, let's talk about how you might broach the conversation because for many, starting the conversation is the hardest part. Try this on for size:

"I'd like to speak with you when you have a moment about a situation that occurred. I'm interested in your perspective, and would like to share mine, as well."

This approach demonstrates you're not just interested in getting your point across, but you're prepared to listen to theirs.

Let's say your boss has a habit of interrupting you in meetings, and yesterday your boss interrupted you again in front of your team when you were in the middle of sharing an idea. You never want to say things like, "You don't respect my opinion", "It was rude when you...", or "You don't value what I have to say." Those are assumptions and opinions.

Instead, use the SBI model:

Situation: "Yesterday in the team meeting, I started to explain my idea for the new product launch."

Behavior: "I hadn't finished my thought when you began to share the update about the marketing vendors. I felt it important to mention, as this has happened on two prior occasions in team meetings."

Impact: "I'm concerned this undermines my credibility with the team."

An important element for this to work well is to continue to loop back into the SBI model if the recipient is not receiving the feedback. Imagine your manager responds defensively by saying, "No one will think anything of it. You're over-reacting."

Using the SBI model:

"Tom, approaching you with this feedback today is not easy or comfortable for me and I gave it considerable thought beforehand {situation}. Your response that I'm over-reacting minimizes the affect these interruptions have on me {behavior} and does not make me feel confident I can have open, honest communication with you, which is critical to our working relationship {impact}."

Give the SBI model a try, even with a spouse, or friend. Remember, people treat you the way you allow them to treat you: an ounce of prevention is worth a pound of cure.

Give neutral, objective feedback

It's crucial to omit assumptions in feedback. "You're trying to…", or "You did this because …", or, "I know you think/feel that…" etc. Unless you're a mind reader, stay far from assumptions and reference observable behavior only.

An assumption of motive might look like this:

"It really bothered me when you reassigned my project to Ellen. It concerns me *you don't trust me* to do my job."

If that is not truly the motive, the other person may become irritated or develop hurt feelings about your assumptions of what they think or how they feel.

An approach like this is more likely to be effective:

"Reassigning the Acme project to another team member without sharing the rationale has left me wondering if I've done something to lose your trust. Can you help me understand the reason behind the decision?"

This tactic is more likely to elicit a compassionate or a reasonable response, rather than a defensive reaction.

No hyperbole, please.

Magnifications and over statements such as, "You never...", or "You always..." are problematic. First, they aren't accurate – they're an exaggeration. Second, they're antagonistic, setting the stage for feedback to be ignored because people know they don't *always* or *never* do anything. Hyperbole weakens credibility of your feedback, and perhaps you, if this approach is consistent.

Calmly handle resistance

If you have provided objective, verbal feedback in a calm, neutral tone, at an appropriate time and place, referencing only observable behavior, it's harder for someone to respond poorly.

However, if your feedback is met with rejection, I recommend the following approach:

- Explain that providing feedback was difficult, you reflected on the situation prior to coming to them, and you're concerned their reaction will make it harder to come to them and have open communication in the future. You could also add you believe positive conflict resolution is important for the effectiveness of your working relationship.
- Remain silent. Maintain eye contact. Wait for a response.
- If they respond favorably and soften, you've been successful!
- If they continue defensively, explain your perception of the situation still remains. Ask for their opinion on how the situation should be resolved. Remain silent. Maintain eye contact. Wait for a response.
- If they continue to respond negatively, simply thank them for their time and part company.
- In a work context, document the conversation, its outcome, including their response to the suggested resolution, using exact phrases if possible. One idea is to send an email to the person, with a summary of the conversation and its outcome.
- Follow up a couple of days later and ask them if they've had time to reflect on the discussion, and if anything has changed. You want to allow them time to come around if they were having a bad day, or going through something you were unaware of.
- If the original situation was serious (e.g., you were giving feedback about inappropriate behavior) and their stance has not changed, consider escalating to Human

Resources or the person's manager, along with your documentation of the conversation (which, in their own words, will demonstrate their unwillingness to resolve conflict).

Some people cannot admit their mistakes. You may have to cut your losses with these people, but don't assume they aren't coachable until you try. Unwillingness to accept feedback will catch up to them eventually.

Learning to Read People to Increase Understanding

To successfully interact with people, meet their needs, and understand what motivates them requires knowing how to read and adapt to others.

Learning to read people becomes easier if you know what to look for, and it's a professional advantage. It requires three things: identification, observation, and practice.

As a human behavior consultant and career coach, it's common for me to have conversations with my clients where I end up coaching them on an interpersonal conflict – it's sometimes the primary driver for clients seeking career services. Learning to read and manage different personalities has been instrumental in drastically minimizing my own conflict with others.

Identifying Personality Style

Earlier in the book I provided an overview of the DiSC four-factor personality model. Let's expand on those concepts and how you can leverage them to better communicate with people.

There are three cues for identifying personality: facial expression, hand gestures, and verbal cues.

Facial Expression

When talking to someone, how much do they smile?

- Abundant smiles suggests an **I** or **S** style
- Only socially required smiles, such as being introduced, indicates a **D** or **C** style

Hand Gestures

How animated are the person's hand gestures and body movement?

- Slow hand gestures which are close to body indicates a **C** or **S** style
- Fast gestures that extend away from body indicate a **D** or **I** style

Verbal Cues

How fast does the person speak, and do they interrupt?

- A slower-paced speaker who stops speaking when interrupted indicates an **S** or **C** style
- A fast-paced speaker that doesn't stop speaking when interrupted indicates a **D** or **I** style

How much small talk?

- Making small talk (e.g., talks about personal life) indicates an **I** or **S** style
- Sticking to task-oriented work topics indicates a **D** or **C** style

How can you tell if a person that smiles a lot is an I or S style? Look at the hand gestures!

- Slow/close to body is an **S** style
- Fast and away from body is an **I** style

How can you tell if a person that talks fast and interrupts is a D or I style?

- If they are engaging in "small-talk" and smiling, they are an **I** style
- If they stick to task-related topics and are not smiling in the conversation, they are likely a **D** style

Simple Techniques to Improve Communication

> "Life would be easy if it weren't for other people"
> – CONNIE PODESTA

Because of different personalities, we connect with some people more easily than others.

- 90% of problems at work are people problems.
- A significant cause of terminations are personality issues.
- A difficult co-worker can negatively impact satisfaction in the workplace.
- A personality conflict with a manager can make you dread going to work.

**When Communicating with a D
Do...**

- Be clear and to the point
- Start with the bottom line
- Stick to the subject
- Be logical in presenting facts
- Provide options
- Ask pertinent questions
- *Remember:* relationship is secondary to tasks
- Establish time frames; they're result-driven
- Use bulleted, concise writing

Limit These...

- Over friendliness
- Generalizations
- Talking too much
- Repeating yourself
- Making unsupportable statements
- Getting emotional
- Loud or boisterous behavior
- Going off on tangents

**When Communicating with an I
Do...**

- Be open, warm, and friendly
- Concentrate on the people aspect
- Take time, socialize
- Encourage and support enthusiasm
- Be sure a decision is made
- Listen attentively

- Give regular feedback
- Chat over lunch or coffee

Limit These...

- Restricting their time
- Showing a "cold" manner
- Doing all the talking
- Jumping to facts too quickly
- Being brusque
- Restricting their ideas/suggestions
- Looking at your watch

When Communicating with an S
Do...

- Be sincere
- Give warm, personal compliments
- Ask questions, listen
- Show interest in them and their work
- Give assurance
- Make them feel comfortable
- Give them regular feedback
- Discuss versus dictate

Limit These...

- Being overpowering
- Demanding or dominating
- Pushing ideas too aggressively
- Stating too many facts
- Asking closed-ended (yes/no) questions
- Telling them what to do

- Making communication one-way
- Making "casual" promises

When Communicating with a C
Do...

- Take your time
- Have all the facts
- Be organized
- Think "professional" for presentations
- Provide information in writing
- Avoid gimmicks
- Be thorough
- Concentrate on specifics
- Establish a time frame
- Plant seeds; provide information in advance

Limit These...

- Generalize about details
- Be vague
- Act too casual
- Waste time on casual conversation
- Jump around from one point to another
- Jump to the bottom line too quickly
- Force quick decisions on important issues
- Act too familiar
- Assume they will trust quickly
- "Surprises"

Another great application of adaptive communication is a job interview. Using the personality identification tips should help you better connect and communicate with different styles and enhance rapport with interviewers.

I'm not suggesting insincerity, but to demonstrate flexibility when communicating with others in a professional and personable manner. Think of it like this: If you speak loudly to a relative who is hard of hearing even though you're not naturally loud, it doesn't mean you're being fake. You're just attempting to communicate with them effectively.

Let's look at a few more communication strategies:

To Connect Better with the D Style

Address issues quickly and directly. They will respect you for it.
Resist the urge to give into their demands just to regain harmony.
Avoid taking bluntness personally. It's not personal.
Focus on the big picture.
Expect candor.
Make efficient use of their time: Be brief. Be gone!

To Connect Better with the S Style

Show warmth and concern for their feelings.
Address the situation directly, but avoid being confrontational.
Offer your point of view, but take an easy-going approach.
Work collaboratively with them.
Respect their cautious pace.
Set a timeline that fits everyone's needs.
Avoid forceful tactics.
Show them you sincerely care about resolving the issues.

To Connect Better with the I Style

Be open to collaboration.
Recognize value in their energy and enthusiasm.
Find ways to recognize them so they feel liked and appreciated.
Expect spontaneity.
Show them you're open to creative solutions.
Remain optimistic while considering all potential issues.
Let them know your relationship is solid despite differences.
Avoid personal attacks.
Acknowledge their feelings.

To Connect Better with the C Style

Allow them time for careful analysis.
Talk to them about objective, fact-based aspects of ideas and projects.
Support your opinions with logic and facts.
Avoid using forceful or emotional tactics.
Give them space to process a situation before confronting the issues.
Show appreciation for their logic.
Expect skepticism.
Avoid pressuring them for an immediate decision.

The most common coping mechanisms people use for personality conflict are avoidance, passive aggressive behavior, and permanently leaving the situation. The challenge with these strategies is avoidance and passive-aggressive behavior worsens the relationship.

There will likely be people you don't hit it off with in your next environment, and you can't continually flee from conflict because there are always going to be people you struggle to get along with naturally.

A more effective strategy is learning to understand people, and adapting your approach to give others what they need, and ultimately get your needs met in the process.

The poet John Donne wrote:

No man is an island,

Entire of itself,

Every man is a piece of the continent,

A part of the main.

Regardless of your job, everything is accomplished with or through people. The ability to build trust, fulfill the needs of others and self through relationship, and successfully interact with a variety of people and personalities is a sound investment that will pay dividends in improved interpersonal success in every area of your life.

Success Strategy # 3: Building Strong Relationships

RV Rhodes, the company my mother founded, is headquartered in Buffalo, NY. When I took a job at the University of Buffalo, it was the first time I worked in or around the city of Buffalo.

I met so many people coming through the School of Management who knew my mother. Often she had coached them, consulted with their company, was a fellow member of *Leadership Buffalo,* or had served on a board with them.

At the time, it was a little embarrassing to have people walk up to me and say, "You're Judi's daughter? I love your mom!"

As I got older, I began to realize the value of her reputation. My mother told me 80% of coaches (executive, career, life) fail in the first year. Of those who succeed, only 20% earn six-figure salaries. And of those earning six figures, just 2% are women.

My mother's ability to build strong relationships is one of the primary reasons she made it into the 2% of women who earn six figures as coaches. Her business was entirely word of mouth, and the strong relationships she built meant that people advocated her services. Her legacy will be a person who was always giving.

The WISE profile defines *Building Strong Relationships* as: "The ability to successfully interact with one or more persons, build trust and fulfill psychological and emotional needs of others, and self, so all parties derive value from the relationship. Understanding what motivates others and how to build alliances based in shared goals and beliefs."

Givers have better relationships than takers

When I think of giving, I think of kindness, reciprocated sharing and caring, and doing favors and good deeds for others.

When I was a very young adult I thought if I died, very few people would likely attend my funeral. I realize that's a strange thing to ponder, but it wasn't the lack of turn out that troubled me, it was what it represented – it meant I wasn't positively affecting people's lives the way I should be.

I continue to see the value my mother brings to people's lives. Recognizing I wasn't making a difference for others the way I should is what prompted me to change. I began serving at church, and offered to help people when I was presented with a need I was able to meet, instead of convincing myself I was too busy to help.

Do you want your life to be characterized by sharing, caring, doing favors and good deeds? Here are some ways to give:

- Volunteer in your area of expertise or skill.
- Write a blog offering free advice on a subject where you are knowledgeable.
- Contact organizations that pair your passions with charities serving that need, such as *OneBrick.org*.[9]
- Donate time to efforts such as Operation Christmas Child, or your local food bank when they are especially busy such as the weeks leading up to Thanksgiving and Christmas.

Volunteer work is a win-win. It will give you a stronger sense of purpose, increase your network, and help you form new skills.

How to Win Friends and Influence People
Dale Carnegie noted six simple and effective ways to connect better relationally in his timeless book, *How to Win Friends and Influence People*.

1. *Become genuinely interested in other people.* One effective strategy is to ask questions to learn more about the person. e.g. "Where are you from?", "What are your hobbies?", "What is your favorite vacation spot?"

2. *Smile.* People think of others who smile as more confident and successful, and are more likely to strike up conversation with someone who smiles. It's also a stress-reliever!

3. *Remember a person's name is, to that person, the sweetest and most important sound in any language.* When meeting someone, repeat their name back to them – "It's nice to meet you, Jenna." Also, if you form a connection of their name with something familiar, you're more likely to remember it.

4. *Be a good listener.* Encourage others to talk about themselves rather than playing the "all about me" track when speaking with someone.

5. *Talk in terms of the other person's interests.* People will enjoy conversing with you when you talk about what interests them, rather than only what interests you (your job, kids, and opinions).

6. *Make the other person feel important – and do it sincerely.* The best way to make a person feel important is to focus on them and what they have to say. In addition, expressing genuine interest and enthusiasm toward them goes a long way.

How often do you practice these timeless tips? I recommend selecting one tip to start practicing. It may feel uncomfortable at first, but it will get easier!

Strong relationships are built on one foundation: *trust.*

Another excellent resource to build strong relationships is the book, *The Collaboration Breakthrough: Think Differently. Achieve More.* The authors include a tool called the *5 Confidence Factors.* It describes attributes that drive confidence and trust among co-workers: competence, openness, reliability, fairness, and caring, including a free confidence assessment. Visit *www.collaboration-breakthrough.com* for more information.

Success Strategy # 4: Life-long Learning

One of the underlying themes in my mom's career story is her self-described "sponge" learning behavior. And this behavior was not limited to the workplace.

When I was young I would often ask my mother what an unfamiliar word meant and she'd encourage me to find a dictionary to look up the definition. I began watching television with a dictionary close by, and got hooked on reading the dictionary in my spare time.

My mother's thirst for knowledge stoked a love of learning in my own heart. I remember going to the library on Saturday where I would pore over the reference books you weren't permitted to check out. I especially loved books about maps, science, and animals.

One of the most exciting days of my childhood was when I turned 12 and obtained an adult library card, and could check out as many books as I wanted. I would lug my rented treasures home, spread them all over my bed, and marvel at the endless facts at my fingertips.

The life-long learning my mother taught me changed my work life.

After my oldest son was born, I took a job at the University of Buffalo's School of Management in the Executive MBA program. Because I worked at the school, I was able to audit courses for free.

I decided to take a 10-week Human Resources program, and a 10-week Micro-MBA program to grow in new areas. While I was there, I also taught myself how to update information on the Executive MBA website, and create Access databases.

I'll never forget the pivotal day in my career just after I started a new customer service role at TeleTech, at a customer contact center. An HR leader knocked on the door of my class and pulled me out of training to see the site's senior IT leader – an intimidatingly large man with tattoos on his forearms. I was in my 20s and to me, he looked like he'd been a marine before joining Corporate America.

He asked me to sit down and handed me a job description for an Intranet Developer position, a web application programming job. Apparently, the HR leader noticed I had updated webpages in my previous position, and passed my resume along to him.

Updating content on webpages was nothing at all like programming. I was grossly unqualified which was a snap for me to determine because what were these things in the job description called ADO, SQL, VB, or JavaScript, anyway?

I thanked him for his time, and said I was very flattered but I wasn't qualified for the position. Then I went back to the training class.

The next day, the IT leader himself pulled me out of class, and asked me to come to his office. I'll never forget what he said to me in that meeting. He told me my resume demonstrated I was a person who wanted to continually learn. He looked me straight in the eye and said, "I'm not asking you if you're qualified for this job. I'm asking if you think you can *learn* it."

I sat for a moment in silence, thinking of what I'd just heard. I had never taken a computer class in my life, let alone programming. After thinking for a moment, I responded, "Well, when you put it that way, yes. I can learn just about anything."

I never went back to the customer representative training class, and continued to work in IT in technical roles for the next 11 years.

McMurray defines life-long learning this way: "Being endlessly curious about a broad spectrum of topics. Having an insatiable appetite for knowledge through both formal and informal learning opportunities that facilitate the continuous improvement of a woman's professional development and personal fulfillment. Continually stretching oneself and seeking to broaden horizons."

My mother's story and my own illustrate the practice of life-long learning can open unexpected doors.

How often have you heard people complain about being asked to do things that aren't in their job description, or grumble about doing work without the title or compensation to go along with it?

My mother was happy to learn anything her boss was willing to allow. She viewed it as an investment in herself, and that life-long learning has been characteristic throughout her life. If she insisted on staying within the bounds of her receptionist job description, she would have only learned the skills of being a receptionist in her years at PBB.

Instead, the skills reorganizing processes, organizing information, learning shorthand, and others, soon paved the way for her to step into her next role as assistant to a senior executive.

The Power of Yet

Carol Dweck is the Lewis and Virginia Eaton Professor of Psychology at Stanford University. She graduated from Barnard College in 1967 and earned a Ph.D. from Yale University in 1972.

Dweck has built a body of research on the incredible results that can be achieved from a single mental shift from fixed thinking, to a growth mindset. A growth mindset is a key building block of a life-long learner.

This mindset shift caused Native American kids at the bottom of their school district to outperform kids in affluent areas of Seattle. Her Ted talk, using compelling examples, explains how retraining one's thinking in one simple, fundamental way changes how you approach life's challenges.

Following is a humorous endorsement Dweck once received in support of her research:

"I received a letter recently from a 13-year-old boy. He said:

'Dear Professor Dweck, I appreciate that your writing is based on solid scientific research, and that's why I decided to put it into practice. I put more effort into my schoolwork, into my relationship with my family, and into my relationship with kids at school, and I experienced great improvement in all of those areas. I now realize I've wasted most of my life.'"

If only we all could learn such powerful lessons by age 13!

Early in her career, Dweck heard about a college in Chicago where high school students received a grade of *not yet* if they did not pass all of their required courses. This idea fascinated her because she realized it gave these students a path to the future, instead of slamming a door shut in their faces.

Dweck decided to research how children cope with challenge. She presented challenges to 10 year olds that were slightly harder than they were able to solve.

Some of these children responded in a surprisingly positive way. They expressed enthusiasm toward the problems, citing their love of a challenge. These kids believed their abilities could be developed beyond their present capabilities.

Other students reacted disastrously to the problems. They felt their intelligence was being judged, and they failed. These types of students, in study after study, ran from difficulty.

Her research has shown a growth mindset alters the way people view setbacks or failure. Instead of a fatalistic view of failure, a growth mindset creates greater persistence.

We are always learning on a continuum, where we are following an upward trajectory of learning through challenges, and rather than believing our skills, abilities, and intelligence are *fixed*, we see challenges as opportunities toward growth beyond our current capabilities.

Recently, a friend of mine told me a story about butterflies. She said butterflies struggle and thrash against the walls of their cocoon in order to break out, and if you tear open the cocoon to make it easy for the butterfly to escape, their wings are under-developed and they never learn to fly. The result is they die, either by starvation or being eaten.

The lesson? There is growth in struggle.

Do you have a fixed mindset or a growth mindset? What about those around you? Do you see a correlation between those with fixed mindsets, and their self-imposed, limited success?

It seems funny that a 13-year-old can understand the power of Carol Dweck's research, and the discipline to implement it. So did my mom. What about you?

To learn more about, watch Carol S. Dweck's *The Power of Yet* Tedx Talk on YouTube.[10]

Success Strategy # 5: Being a Risk Taker

People who are especially talented in risk-taking are comfortable with ambiguity, take a rational approach to decision-making, and embrace challenges enthusiastically.

Re-entering the workforce after a long absence carries risk.

Quitting your job is a risk.

Asking for things you want may be a risk.

Stepping out in a new career direction is a risk.

Starting your own business is a risk.

My mother took a risk in all of these areas. Each time she was willing to step away from solid ground and into uncharted waters, leading her one step closer to a fulfilling career.

Moms always seem to have these wise sayings we end up adopting as we get older. One of the things my mom always says is, "Nothing that is worth something is ever easy." It reminds me of the Chinese proverb, "Pearls don't reside on the shore. If you want one, you must dive for it."

The WISE Profile defines *Being a Risk Taker* as: "Being ok with working outside of one's comfort zone, setting stretch goals and seeking out challenges for the sake of professional and personal development. Consciously controlled behavior with a perceived uncertainty about its outcome, which has the potential outcome of failure, yet also provides the opportunity for an outcome that can be positive and further goals."

It's not natural for everyone to be risk-takers. In fact, our brain is wired to protect us, so any time we consider doing something we think may be risky our brain immediately tries to shield us from harm through self-doubt or thoughts that talk us out of taking a risk.

Many of us struggle with fear and self-doubt, and these thoughts of doubt and failure leave us stuck in neutral.

Calculated Risk-Taking

Willingness to take risk does not promote recklessness. Risk simply implies you can't be 100% certain of the outcome; the potential for both failure and reward exists.

You will never be completely comfortable when taking a risk because comfort is safety, and safety is the domain of underachievement.

Should You Work for Yourself?

Self-employment isn't for everyone. Some personalities enjoy the routine, structure, and perceived stability of being someone's employee. Others feel like a caged animal.

Those who dream of working for themselves but don't take the leap often fear they won't generate enough income to live; a reasonable concern. Here's something interesting to consider:

A team of researchers once followed a group of 1,500 people over a period of 20 years. At the beginning of the study, the participants were placed in two groups.

Group A, 83% of the sample, were people who chose a career path based solely on the prospect of making money now in order to do what they wanted later in life.

Group B, the remaining 17%, were people who selected a career path to do what they wanted now, and indicated they would worry about money later.

At the end of 20 years, 101 of the 1,500 people became millionaires. Of the millionaires, 100 out of 101 were from Group B – the group that pursued what they loved.[11]

Ask yourself, "What would I do if money was no object?" and check out Allan Watt's You Tube video: *What if Money Was No Object?* [12]

Perhaps passion isn't a motivator for you. Maybe you're a person who needs more solid confirmation to decide if you should take the plunge into your own business.

I've coached a number of people who just can't seem to fall in line with being an employee and it's usually because they have a strong entrepreneurial bent. They sometimes describe themselves as "terrible employees." Instead of helping them find a job, I help them identify steps toward self-employment.

To some, the thought of starting a business can be exciting, scary, daunting, and thrilling. If you've found limited satisfaction in your career and feel a strong pull to go your own way, maybe it's time to spread your wings and fly!

The Gallup organization has identified the top 10 talents of highly successful entrepreneurs. It's unlikely you will possess all 10 strongly, but you can find out your dominant talents, and where you'd likely need some support to ensure success.

The 10 entrepreneurial talents are:

Confidence

Determination

Disruptor

Profitability

Selling

Risk-Taker

Independent

Knowledge-Seeker

Delegator

Relationship-Builder

Tips for Risk Taking

- Learn to work outside your comfort zone by setting stretch goals and seeking out challenges.
- Grow your ability and knowledge to calculate the positives and negatives of taking chances/risks toward building your career.
- Use this free Risk Impact/Probability Tool offered by MindTools® to work through risk, impact, and risk mitigation options to increase your probability of success. *https://www.mindtools.com/pages/article/newPPM_78.htm*

Check out other tools in the *Additional Tools & Resources* section of the book, including a Risk Impact/Probability chart with a downloadable worksheet and tips for creating contingency plans.

These tools will help you identify likely risks you may face, assess their likelihood and estimated impact, and develop a planned response.

What is a risk you've been afraid to take?

> "The best time to plant a tree was 20 years
> ago. The second best time is now."
> — CHINESE PROVERB

Assess Yourself!

The WISE Profile (Women's Inventory for Success Empowerment)
Now that you've learned about each of the five success factors
correlated to success in women, which strongly contributed to
my mom's career success and satisfaction, the next thing you
may want to do is assess where your strength and development
opportunities are within each of these factors.

The best way to assess yourself on the career success factors
is using the WISE Profile, developed by Valerie McMurray. The
WISE Profile enables women to gain insights to help them navigate the challenges in their career so they can achieve maximum
career and leadership potential. No matter what stage of your
career, this assessment will bring valuable awareness to your competency level against the five critical career and leadership success factors.

The WISE Profile includes ideas for actions you can take
to increase your effectiveness in specific areas within the five
factors.

I've always viewed myself a learner, but my results on the
WISE Profile revealed:

My **overall** score for Life-long Learning is **5.9**. The scale is 1
to 10, with 5 being the mid-point. The range of scores for Life-
long Learning is 3.5 - 8.2, meaning no one who has taken the assessment has scored lower than 3.5, or higher than 8.2 (extreme
scores are rare).

Has an insatiable appetite for learning: **7.4**
Continually stretches oneself: **5.0**
Strives to grow professionally through continuous study: **5.7**
Continuously seeks to broaden professional horizons: **5.6**

As you can see, I have a strong appetite for learning (score
of 7.4) but prefer to learn things within my comfort zone, where
I have strong interest. I'm less inclined to stretch outside my

comfort zone (score of 5.0). I know this to be true. In college, I signed up for Statistics, when Calculus was going over my head. When I'm interested, I pursue something doggedly, but I don't have the same drive when I'm lukewarm or disinterested.

If you would like to take the WISE Profile assessment, the present cost of the assessment and a one-hour debrief with a certified WISE coach is $179. Feel free to contact me through my website at *www.virtuscareers.com* to learn more. If you'd like to become certified to administer the WISE Profile at your company, or as an independent consultant, contact Valerie McMurray at *http://www.thenorthstarcg.com/contact/*.

In addition to developing the five career success factors, there are other practical ways to develop your potential, such as participating in mentoring relationships.

In the next section, *Bonus Success Superchargers,* we'll take a closer look at some additional strategies to supercharge your career.

PART 4

Bonus Success Superchargers

Quadrant 2 Living

Have you ever seen the Disney/Pixar movie, *Up?* Spoiler alert! It's a story about Carl and Ellie - childhood friends who fall in love and get married. They have a dream to visit Paradise Falls in Venezuela, and begin saving for the trip in a glass jar. Over the course of their lives Carl repeatedly breaks the jar open to pay for car repairs, hospital bills, and a variety of other unexpected expenses. Before long, they've reached old age, still without visiting Paradise Falls, and we witness a heart-wrenching scene of unfulfilled dreams with Ellie sick in the hospital.

If you've never seen the movie or would like a refresher, watch a two-minute clip on YouTube: *https://youtu.be/2PD7qi8VK_o*

Carl reflects on the dream that's taken a backseat to the daily demands of life, then he takes a leap. He visits a travel agent, purchases two tickets to Venezuela, and presents them to Ellie in her hospital bed. In the next scene, we see Carl sitting alone in a church after the funeral of his beloved, Ellie. Her life has ended, leaving their dream of visiting Paradise Falls together forever unfulfilled.

There wasn't a dry eye in the house during this scene. Why? Because unrealized dreams are a universal human experience and there is something profoundly disappointing and sad when we realize a dream is forever lost.

Many live like Carl and Ellie, postponing the pursuit of our passion and dreams. Why do we do this? What's the difference between people who realize their dreams, and those who don't? At the core, it's one behavior: Living in Quadrant 2, introduced by the late Stephen Covey (*Figure 3a*).

Figure 3a

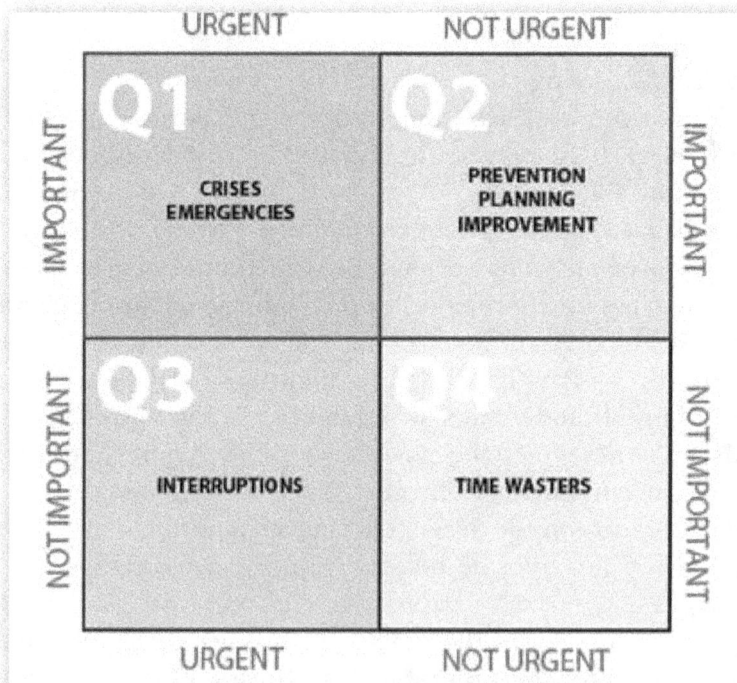

Image credit: Alex Czartoryski

How we spend our time boils down to importance (low/ high) and urgency (low/high). Not everything that is urgent is important. Not everything that is important is urgent.

When we focus on the urgent, we fill our time with busy work and time wasters, and leave little-to-no time for the important, which is the place where prevention, planning, and improvement lives; in essence, the behaviors that lead to goal fulfillment.

- Q1: Important and Urgent – Crises and Emergencies
- Q2: Important but Not Urgent – Prevention, Planning, Improvement
- Q3: Not Important but Urgent – Interruptions and Busy Work
- Q4: Not Important and Not Urgent – Time Wasters

Spending our lives on what's urgent instead of what's important is why we neglect family time for the sake of work, why we don't take "me" time, and why we struggle to find time to exercise or invest in our personal and professional development.

People who achieve their dreams spend time in Quadrant 2: important, but not urgent. They don't relegate their dreams to the back seat, letting time wasters, interruptions, and busy work drive their lives.

How do you start living in Quadrant 2 today?

- Set smaller personal goals that will incrementally lead to your ultimate goal.
- Plan time each week for Quadrant 2 activities that lead to reaching your goal.
- Be uncompromising. Defend that sacred time. This means saying no to people when they attempt to drag you into other quadrants.

Since I was in my 20s I longed to have my own coaching business. When I moved into my 40s, I started my business, but kept one foot in Corporate America. I was tired from working so much, but wasn't willing to put both feet solidly into my business.

In February 2015, I decided to set a specific goal. Each weekend I carved out time, no matter what was going on, to the fulfillment of my goal of writing this book. If someone told me I'd write a book while raising two teenagers, a two-year old, launching a business while working full-time, and investing in my marriage, I'd have called you crazy. If you commit to Quadrant 2 living, you can reach your goals.

Don't tell me you don't have time! You have as many hours in a day as every other person who has achieved greatness. How are you spending your time?

In June 2015, I quit my corporate job to focus solely on my coaching business. That single goal, and setting time each weekend to reach it, is why I'm my own boss today.

So, you see, I'm not trying to sell you some nice-sounding theory. Purposeful time management will lead you to bigger and better things in your life. I hope I've encouraged you to make a change, starting today!

Developing Your Critical Thinking Skills

Earlier in the book, when I introduced you to the concept of the Human Iceberg, I presented critical thinking skills as the best way to solve problems, draw conclusions from information, make inferences from data, and separate assumption from fact.

The Foundation for Critical Thinking offers an excellent, practical approach to developing critical thinking skills.[13]

First, recognize there are six critical thinking developmental stages:

Stage 1: The Unreflective Thinker (we are unaware of significant problems in our thinking)

Stage 2: The Challenged Thinker (we become aware of problems in our thinking)

Stage 3: The Beginning Thinker (we try to improve but without regular practice)

Stage 4: The Practicing Thinker (we recognize the necessity of regular practice)

Stage 5: The Advanced Thinker (we advance in accordance with our practice)

Stage 6: The Master Thinker (skilled & insightful thinking become second nature to us)

The two prerequisites to advancing across the developmental stages are:

1. Accepting there are serious problems in our thinking, i.e., accept *challenges* to our thinking
2. Regular practice

The Foundation for Critical Thinking offers 9 strategies to increase your critical thinking ability:

Use "Wasted" Time

At the end of the day or at a time when you're prone to time wasters, like flipping through TV channels, repurpose that time for reflection. Ask yourself:

- When did I do my worst thinking today?
- When did I do my best?
- What did I think about today?
- Did I figure anything out?
- Did I allow negative thinking to frustrate me unnecessarily?
- If I had to repeat today what would I do differently? Why?
- Did I do anything today to further my long-term goals?
- Did I act in accordance with my own values?
- If I spent every day this way for 10 years, would I accomplish something worthy of that time?

A Problem a Day

At the beginning of each day choose a problem to work on while you're driving to work, or have a spare moment. Determine the logic of the problem by identifying its elements, i.e., systematically think through the questions: What *is* the problem? How can I put it into the form of a question? How does it relate to my goals, purposes, and needs?

Internalize Intellectual Standards

Each week, develop a heightened awareness of one of the universal intellectual standards: clarity, precision, accuracy, relevance, depth, breadth, logicalness, significance.

Try focusing one week on clarity, the next on accuracy, and so on. For example, if you are focusing on clarity for the week, try to notice when you are being unclear in communicating with others. Notice when others are unclear in what they are saying.

Keep an Intellectual Journal

Each week, write out a certain number of journal entries. Try using this format, keeping each numbered stage separate:

1. Situation – Describe a situation that is, or was, emotionally significant to you. Focus on one situation at a time.
2. Your Response – Describe what you did in response to that situation. Be specific and exact.
3. Analysis – Analyze, in light of what you wrote, what was going on in the situation. Dig beneath the surface.
4. Assessment – Assess the implications of your analysis. What did you learn about yourself? What would you do differently if you could relive the situation?

Reshape Your Character

Choose one trait – e.g., intellectual perseverance, autonomy, empathy, courage, humility – to strive for each month, and how you can develop that trait. For example, concentrating on intellectual humility, notice when you admit you are wrong. Notice when you refuse to admit you are wrong, even in the face of evidence you are in fact wrong.

Notice when you become defensive when another person tries to point out a deficiency in your work, or your thinking.

Notice when your intellectual arrogance keeps you from learning. For example, when do you say to yourself, "I already know everything I need to know about this subject" or "I know as much as he does. Who does he think he is, forcing his opinions on me?" By owning your ignorance, you can begin to deal with it.

Deal with Your Egocentrism

On a daily basis, observe egocentric thinking in action by contemplating:

- Under what circumstances do I think with a bias in favor of myself?
- Did I ever become irritable over small things?

- Did I do or say anything "irrational" to get my way?
- Did I try to impose my will upon others?
- Did I ever fail to speak my mind when I felt strongly about something, and then later feel resentment?

Once you identify egocentric thinking in action, you can replace it with rational thought through self-reflection:

- What would a rational person feel in this or that situation?
- What would a rational person do?
- How does that compare with what I want to do?

Hint: If you find you continually conclude a rational person would behave as you have, you are probably engaging in self-deception.

Redefine the Way You See Things
We live in a world where every situation is "defined," or, given a meaning. How a situation is defined determines not only how we feel about it, but how we act in it. However, virtually every situation can be defined in more than one way. This fact implies tremendous opportunity.

In principle, it is within our power to make our lives happier and more fulfilling. Many of the negative definitions we give to situations could be transformed into positive ones. We can be happy when otherwise we would have been sad. Fulfilled rather than frustrated.

Get in Touch with Your Emotions
When you feel a negative emotion, ask yourself: What is the thinking leading to this emotion?

If you are angry, ask yourself: what is the thinking that is making me angry? What other ways could I think about this situation?

Can you think about the situation to see humor in it, or what is pitiable in it? If you can, concentrate on that thinking and your emotions will eventually shift to match it.

Analyze Group Influences on Your Life

Reflect on behavior which is encouraged, and discouraged, in the groups you belong. Every group enforces some level of conformity. For any given group, what are you required to believe? What are you forbidden to do? Most people live too much within the view of themselves projected by others. Discover what pressure you are bowing to and think explicitly about whether or not to reject that pressure.

As you continue to test these strategies and build on them in your day-to-day life, you will discover interesting insights that lead to growth through discovery.

Learn Effective Time Management

Earlier I introduced you to Quadrant 2 living. Here are some additional strategies to learn to better manage your time. Please don't skip this step. Few people have proper boundaries that demonstrate their value for their time.

There are five pressures that derail people. Time, or lack of it, is one (the others are relationships, money, health issues, and expectations). Time is fixed; there are only 24 hours in a day. The only thing that can change is you, and what's on your plate.

- People who are **skilled** at managing time use it effectively and efficiently. They *value* their time, concentrate their efforts on more important priorities, get more done in less time than others, and can attend a wider range of activities.

- People who are **unskilled** at managing time waste it. They flit from activity to activity with little rhyme or reason, don't set priorities, can't say no, are easily distracted, don't follow a plan or method, and don't control time wasters.

If the unskilled definition sounds more like you, don't lose hope. Read on.

Calculate what the hours and minutes of your time are worth by using your gross salary, overhead, and benefits. Ask yourself, is what I'm about to do worth $121 dollars of my time? Look at your calendar to see where your biggest time wasters are coming from. How much can you reduce these activities? Could you reduce them by 50%?

- Are you participating in meetings where you don't need to be there?
- Batch activities together where possible.
- Use your most productive and alert time of day for the toughest projects, not the easy tasks.
- Make a list of points to make before you place a call to stay on task.

Delegate

If you are a people leader, give yourself needed margin by delegating away some tasks. Delegation provides stretch opportunities for others, creates bench strength for your team, and frees you to focus on higher priorities. Others feel empowered when they are given stretch assignments.

Keep it Brief

Do you value other people's time? Are you guilty of talking beyond what is necessary when meeting with co-workers? Do the people around you respect your time?

Learn to say: "I have to get back to my next task. Can we pick this up another time?"

Say No

You are always going to be asked to do more than you're able.

The best time saver is learning to constructively say no. An effective technique is to ask what can be canceled or delayed to make way for this new priority. This allows you to say yes, but you're also saying no to something of the requester's choice. They may choose to delegate to someone with more capacity to take the work on.

Plan up Front

It sounds counter-intuitive to add planning to your plate and end up with more time, but it works!

Up-front planning of priorities frees up more time down the road than just arbitrarily tackling everything you can. Recent research reveals people who work more than 50 hours a week are less productive than their counterparts. Take time to renew. It helps you refocus so that you can be at your best. Stephen Covey calls this *sharpening the saw.*

People tend to focus on work they like and end up under the gun doing unsavory tasks under pressure. Allocate your time evenly toward desirable, as well as undesirable, tasks. Put tasks on your calendar for a specific time instead of simply listing it on a task list.

Create and incorporate goals into your planning. Separate them by importance/priority:

- Mission critical
- Important
- Nice to have
- If there is time left over
- Not central to what I am trying to achieve

You can also create time goals. For example, you can plan to spend an hour each day on an important task.

Finally, learn from others. Do you know someone who seems to juggle everything in their life flawlessly? Learn their secret sauce to time management and apply the principles to your own life.

Time is too precious to waste. Take control today and watch your life change for the better.

Avoid Joy Killers

As you invest in your career development, your mental attitude is critical to success. The career path is bound to have set backs from time to time, and maintaining a positive perspective is key to perseverance.

Shawn Achor, author of *The Happiness Advantage*, suggests 90% of long-term happiness is predicted not by what happens in the world, but by the way your brain *processes* the world.[14] Perspective is everything!

Beware joy killers. These 7 mental traps will yank the joy out of you:

Disappointment

It's human to feel disappointed. I once applied for a job I wanted and felt qualified for, but wasn't even contacted for an interview. I was so disappointed, because I knew I could excel and it would take my career in an exciting new direction.

When I allow my unmet expectations to govern my satisfaction with my life, I have to reexamine my expectations.

Are they within my control or influence? So many times we have expectations that are blocked, by others or circumstances, which leads to frustration. When our expectations are impossible because they depend on variables we can't control, it leads to depression. Looking back on that job, I later learned the department had a very work-hard (but not play-hard) culture.

It would not have been a good fit for me at that time in my personal life. If I'd been offered that job, I may not have started my own coaching business, which ultimately is the best career fit for me.

> **The antidote?** Focus your energy on what is within your *ability or right* to control (this does not include other people), and reframe your expectations accordingly.

Negative voices

I could go on a tangent (but I won't!) on how imperative it is to silence your constant inner critic. Negative thoughts create feelings of anxiety and stress, and cause your sympathetic nervous system to release fight or flight neurochemicals.

When your body enters this state, blood flows away from your pre-frontal cortex (the part of the brain that deals with reason, analysis, and strategy) to aid your body in a fight or flight response to stress.

This dampens our creativity and resilience, and reduces our ability to reason by one-third our normal capacity. This is why people say and do irrational things when they're upset, because the part of the brain that deals with the ability to be rational is impaired.

> **The antidote?** Play a new track in your mind about your identity using positive adjectives with a focus on your strengths.

Worry

The majority of worry is rooted in future events that never take place. You know the saying: "Worry is like a rocking chair. It gives you something to do, but it doesn't get you anywhere."

What's worse is our brain lies to us when we worry. I had a client who was laid off and living in fear. He said he was tired of being afraid, so I asked him to name exactly what it was that caused his fear. He said if he didn't get a job he wasn't sure what would happen to his family, and his loved ones would be disappointed in him.

I reframed what he said into this statement, and he confirmed this was the root of his worry: "If I don't find work, my family will end up homeless, and will be disappointed in my failure to provide for them."

I asked him to consider an alternative belief: "If I don't find work, family and friends who care about us will help us in our time of need, just as we would help them. My family loves me and will stand by me because they know I'm working hard to find a new position."

Finally, I asked him which statement is most likely to be true of the two – he chose the second.

> **The antidote?** Challenge the truth of your worrisome thoughts. Don't accept them at face value. Byron Katie has a great tool called the *One Belief at a Time* worksheet. You can find this in the *Additional Tools & Resources* section of the book to challenge and overcome negative thoughts and beliefs.

Comparison

There will always be those who have more money, better looks, a fitter figure, a bigger house, smarter kids, and more toys than you do, just as there are people with much less than you have.

Facebook is the ultimate platform for people to parade the highlight reel of their better lives. I'm not here to tell you their life isn't as grand as it seems, though it probably isn't. I'm here to say, "Who cares!?"

The antidote? Gratitude.

Love your partner, love being single, appreciate what you have, your skills, and who you are.

The research on gratitude is conclusive: people who are grateful are happier and healthier (source: John Templeton Foundation). Grateful people will:

- Have 10% fewer stress-related illnesses
- Be more physically fit
- Have blood pressure that is lower by 12%

This research has also shown gratitude increases with age. For every 10 years, gratitude increases by 5%. Overall positive emotions have been shown to add an average of 7 years to one's life.

Your brain can't focus on a positive and a negative simultaneously. Choose gratitude!

Isolation

Some people isolate themselves when going through hard times, but that does not help matters.

My brain-based success instructor told me about research that demonstrated that hugging or holding the hand of a loved one during a difficult time releases oxytocin in your brain, which creates feelings of healing, trust, and love.

The antidote? Surround yourself with supportive people that care about you, and resist the urge to go it alone during tough times.

Unwillingness to forgive

There's a large body of research on the topic of forgiveness. Forgiving someone doesn't mean you're giving them a pass to hurt you again. You can forgive someone and still choose to escort them from your life. Forgiveness means letting go of the root of bitterness planted firmly in your heart.

You can tell if you've forgiven someone by the reaction you have when they walk in a room, or their name comes up in conversation. If you have a negative emotional reaction, the root of bitterness is still alive and putting down deep roots within you.

Unwillingness to forgive creates a toxic soup of negative chemicals that course through your body.

The antidote? Let go and move on from the pain someone has caused you. If you're staying hurt, you're allowing that to happen, not them. Remember, you've hurt others in your life-time, too. Recognize that forgiveness is in *your* best interest, not theirs.

Living contrary to your values

We covered values in detail earlier, and how few things can rob your joy like not being aligned to your values.

The antidote? Research the values of a company before you accept a position. Have courage to speak up if you're asked to do something you don't agree with.

The short-term stress of facing potential conflict for standing up for what you believe in will be dwarfed in comparison to the long-term stress of living against your values daily.

Standing Out at Work

The people I've greatly admired at work stood head and shoulders above the crowd. They were different, and I took notice. So did everyone else, and they experienced professional success. More importantly, they built a reputation that went before them.

These are the kinds of people everyone wants as a mentor. They have a secret sauce, so to speak. Why do they stand out? What are they doing that everyone else isn't? When thinking of this handful of people that influenced my operating principles, I've identified five relatively rare behaviors.

Flawless Follow-through

I once had a co-worker who stood out as someone who took action – especially following through on things that came up in conversation. She stood out because I realized few people are truly proactive.

As an example, I would have a conversation with her and she'd mention some great book she'd read that was related to our topic of conversation. The next morning, that very book would be sitting on my desk with a personal note written on a

post-it inviting me to read and enjoy. Proactive people don't pro-
crastinate. They see opportunities and act.

Bottom line: Be proactive and follow through. Look for
chances to be thoughtful.

Responsiveness

Think about a time you sent an email asking for review or feedback, and received no response. Isn't that frustrating?

Responsive people make time for other people. Instead of
operating in reactive mode, they carve out time to add value to
their own day, as well as those around them. Set aside time each
day to be responsive to people who ask for assistance.

If you can't provide what has been asked of you, be responsive
in saying so. Don't ignore their request. Consider offering some
alternate form of assistance that you can reasonably provide.

Bottom line: Make time to be helpful and responsive.

Adapt to Others

Some of the most impressive people I've worked with who really
stood out know who they are, and adapt their style to others.
Yet, they don't *expect* everyone to adapt to them, and they realize
the impact they have on others when they open their mouth to
speak.

These people take time to discover the needs and priorities
of their co-workers, which enables them to work more effectively
with them. They appreciate the differences in others. They don't
say things like, "I don't have to like you, I just have to work with
you."

Some people value results and action; others prioritize
enthusiasm, stability, accuracy, collaboration, and support.
These self-aware, adaptive people take the time to discover

what their co-workers and customers value, and adapt to meet those needs. They adapt their approach to others. For example, if they have a strong personality, they learn how to temper it to avoid alienating people.

Bottom line: Know yourself, your effect on people, and adapt to others' needs.

Non-defensive

Those who have left a lasting impression on me in my career are people who accept feedback gracefully, and truly have a desire to take a critical look at themselves, based on the feedback of others. Not only were they open to feedback, they thanked me for it, and their behavior changed in response to it.

These people had a non-defensive reaction to constructive feedback and didn't make excuses for themselves. They understand they aren't perfect, and have an attitude of continuous personal improvement that reflects tremendous maturity. It should come as no surprise, then, that Openness to Feedback is one of the five success strategies!

Bottom line: Listen, and be open to feedback.

Attitude of Abundance

An attitude of scarcity is just plain insecurity. Those who operate with a mentality of abundance reap abundance in return. When my mother started her coaching firm, she would often teach other aspiring consultants how to go into business for themselves, sharing her tools, resources, and ideas.

I remember asking her why she was training people to compete with her. I'll never forget her response: "Kristin, my reputation speaks for itself. I have an attitude of abundance, and I don't ever need to feel threatened."

Wow. That attitude has pervaded my thinking thanks to her powerful example. As the saying goes: *Clenched fists can't receive a blessing.*

Bottom line: Share what you know, and invest in others. Think about the behaviors, attitudes, or traits a person possessed who left a strong, positive impression on you and emulate them.

Managing a Bad Boss
According to Gallup research, 82% of companies hire the wrong people for managerial positions. In short, they're in the wrong role. Gallup also reports only 1 in 10 people have the natural talent to manage others well.

These dismal statistics shed light on why so many employees are eager to flee their manager in search of greener pastures. The trouble is, the probability of your new manager providing that green pasture is low.

Rather than continually fleeing from poor managers, why not help your manager manage you better? If you aren't willing to improve your "managing up" skills, you can't really fault your boss for not improving their "managing down" skills.

Here are some effective ways to manage up:

Proactively let your manager know what you need to be successful
If you're not meeting for a regular one-on-one with your manager, approach them and ask to start meeting with you weekly.

Write down all the things you truly need from your manager that you're not currently getting. Share these needs with your manager in a constructive way in your one-on-one. Be reasonable in what you ask for, and avoid approaching your manager in a critical way.

For example, if your manager isn't helping you set priorities to manage your workload, don't be accusatory – simply ask for assistance with priority and goal setting.

Share your strengths

If you're not sure of your strengths, *take the StrengthsFinder assessment* and share your results with your manager. Suggest some ways to incorporate your strengths into special projects, or your main role.

Explain some of the benefits they'll experience, including an increase in your productivity and quality. Playing to your strengths will also increase your engagement, and reduce your stress.

Be willing to give your manager constructive "actionable" feedback

Many people avoid conflict and won't give feedback to their manager. They often believe it won't help, or will make things worse. How has avoidance been working for you to create a good relationship with your manager so far?

In reality, not addressing issues actually increases conflict, fuels passive aggressive behavior, and undermines your relationship. Avoiding issues in an employee/employer relationship doesn't work any better than it does in a marriage.

Allowing dissatisfaction to fester causes you to give off negative vibes that your manager will pick up on. 55% of communication is body language, so you're likely giving off unconscious cues. Your manager may not even be aware of what they're doing, or not doing, to cause you dissatisfaction.

Giving feedback shows a person you care enough about them to invest in their professional improvement. Feedback given in the right way can actually build deeper professional intimacy.

Try using this framework to provide feedback:

- Briefly explain the situation you experienced, or are currently experiencing
- Address observable actions and behavior: leave out your interpretations of the behavior, accusations, or assumptions of motive
- Briefly explain the impact the situation or behavior are having on you, but don't take on a victim posture, or whine – come across as objective and mature
- Suggest an alternative approach for the future

Here's an example:

"I've been struggling with trying to prioritize my workload with the number of projects on my plate. Yesterday when I was assigned the quarterly analysis of our customer feedback data I felt a bit overwhelmed not knowing where all my active projects fit on the priority scale. It would really help me if we could meet weekly for a project prioritization session so I can deliver to your expectations."

If you are unhappy with your manager, try these approaches. Make note of what went well, what could be done better next time, and keep at it. Don't give up if the first attempt is unsuccessful. Relationships are a journey.

Mentoring
Your potential can be turbo-charged simply by having an effective mentor in your life. The best place to be is in the middle of a mentoring sandwich; where you, the mentee, are being mentored by a more experienced person, and you're also mentoring someone.

The beauty of being in the middle is you can teach what you learn from your mentor to your mentee – paying it forward, learning the skill of mentoring while simultaneously being mentored.

There are three basic steps to enter into a mentoring relationship:

1. Identifying potential mentors
2. Making the mentor request
3. Managing the mentoring relationship

How to Identify a Mentor
There are two ways to approach finding a good mentor fit.

You can identify individuals in roles you'd like to be in one day. Or, identify people that possess personal and professional characteristics that you admire and wish to develop.

Making the Mentor Request
When requesting a mentor, you should explain your goals, and why you chose that person as a potential mentor. Let them know the area of expertise or traits you value to provide guidance around potential topics for discussion.

Explain the time commitment you're expecting from this person, and outline what your responsibilities are (more to come on this in a moment). For example, if you expect to speak to your mentor for an hour every other week, let them know so they can make an informed decision based on the time commitment.

When you're asking someone to be your mentor, give them an easy out if they have to say no by stating, "If you're unable to commit to a mentoring relationship, I completely understand.

Based on the goals I've shared would you be able to recommend an alternate mentor if you're unable?"

How to Manage a Mentoring Relationship

A mentee generally has the responsibility to take charge of her own developmental experiences. The mentee is also expected to have ownership over the direction and content of the mentoring relationship.

If you're not sure what to discuss with your mentor, don't worry. A few key questions will help guide your conversation. For your first meeting, talk about each other's expectations and make a formal or informal mentoring agreement to ensure you're both aligned. In the second meeting, you can ask your mentor to share their own career journey, and ask if you may ask questions along the way. This creates an organic conversation to help you understand the path your mentor took to get to the current stage of their career.

Other topics and discussion questions to ask your mentor:

- What difficulties did you encounter in your career? How did you overcome them?
- In your opinion, what have been the key success factors in your career?
- What do you know now, that you wish you knew earlier in your life and career?
- What advice you would offer people who want to make a breakthrough in their career?

Once you've identified areas you'd like to develop, you can also ask your mentor to recommend books, blogs, or other resources to help you develop targeted competencies. Ideally, identifying the competencies required for a desired future role, and assessing your current competency against the target is the best way to identify areas for development.

Mentor Responsibilities

A mentor should honor scheduled appointments, provide quality feedback, and positive development experiences. Some appropriate roles of a mentor are as follows:

- Recommends direction, identifies obstacles, provides coaching to overcome those obstacles
- Provides candid opinions in an open and constructive manner
- Assists in establishing and increasing your professional network
- Promotes and supports your understanding of organizational culture and expectations
- Facilitates discussion, interaction and the exchange of information

Mentee Responsibilities

- Fully participate in the relationship
- Be open to constructive feedback and receive it gracefully
- Schedule meetings and agendas
- Show up on time, prepared for scheduled meetings
- Follow up on action items
- Identify and track goals
- Align key learnings from mentor with your own situation

Development Plans

A development plan is your roadmap to success. It identifies not only your strengths, but areas you'd like to grow and develop to better prepare you for your next career move.

There are a number of ways to approach your development, but here are 10 considerations the global people and organizational advisory firm, Korn Ferry, recommends when creating a development plan:

Choose wisely – Figure out what is critically important to performance in your job or success in your career. Be realistic about what you can accomplish.

Get specific – Get detailed, behavioral feedback on the development need from others. Ask for specific examples. When? Where? With whom? In what settings? Under what conditions? How often?

Identify what you need to start doing, stop doing, and keep doing.

Learn from others – Pick multiple models/mentors whom excel at one thing rather than looking for the "whole package." Identify what they do/don't do down to a set of principles and choose what you wish to integrate into your life.

Read top books on the subject – Buy at least two books covering your need. What are the how-to's on this skill? How is this skill best learned?

Learn from autobiographies and biographies – Learn from famous people who have the skill you are trying to build.

Learn from a course – Find the best courses you have access to, preferably where you not only learn the theory, but have an opportunity to gain practice with the skill.

Try some stretch tasks – 70% of skill development happens on the job. Keep a log of the positive and negative aspects of your performance and note things you will try to do differently or better next time.

Track your progress – Set progress goals and benchmarks for yourself. Celebrate progress! e.g. if you're working on approachability, set a goal to initiate conversation with 5 new people a week.

Get periodic feedback – Leverage people who know you well, and people who haven't known you for a long time.

There are many downloadable sample development plans on-line. You can view several and download a template that works best for you.

Knowing Your Value

A common obstacle to getting where you want to go is an inability to communicate your value. I often recommend to clients they create a value statement, which is similar to an elevator pitch.

Value statements:

- Help you get a firm handle on who you are and what's important to you.
- Set you asucc (most people don't have one).
- Create confidence.
- Are a great way to answer the question, 'Why should I hire or promote you?'
- Provide an opportunity to explain what makes you unique.
- Frame what you're about in networking or exploratory conversations.
- Provide great language for your LinkedIn profile summary.

- Can be used in your resume, and cover letter when competing for new roles and promotions.

Take a look at some example value statements:

"I have confidence, drive and courage to take risks, overcome problems, and take on new ideas. My communication skills, flexibility, adaptability, enthusiasm, and optimism translate to social ease within, and across, teams."

"I'm an innovator. I have a natural tendency to come up with new ideas and combinations of ideas spontaneously to solve complex problems. I'm able to identify solutions that lead to success, and turn those solutions into actionable steps to bring about excellence. My strong communication skills ensure I effectively manage change throughout a transformation."

"I analyze and strategize before I act. In my work, I'm organized and structured. I can be counted upon. I set high standards for myself and I believe I can achieve them. I scan available ideas and concepts, weighing them against a current strategy, and plan for every conceivable contingency."

One might be thinking, "Hey, I own a house cleaning business, and I'm not going to say that when someone asks me what I do for a living."

That's a fair criticism. You should have two versions of your value statement; one spoken, one written.

Here's an example:

John Doe. "What do you do for a living?"

House Cleaner: "I provide white glove cleaning services to help people bring order to their busy lives, and free them up to have more time to focus on what matters to them."

Personally, I'd like to hire a cleaner that expresses purpose in their work, and desires to bring value to my family. It's certainly more compelling than, "I clean houses." The best advice I can give is to create a value statement that is comfortable for you. You're the one who owns it, so it has to feel natural.

Creating your value statement

Make a list of words that are true of you. Using feedback from others, assessments you've taken, and self-evaluation, generate a list of words or short phrases to describe you: e.g., responsible, achievement-oriented, peace-maker, negotiator, idea-generator, problem-solver, accurate, diversity-oriented, safety-conscious, self-confident, learning agile, comfort with ambiguity, motivates others, entrepreneurial, diplomatic, organized.

Cross out words and phrases that are ambiguous or cliché, such as "team player", and choose specific words.

What *makes* you a team player? Are you collaborative? Do you listen well? Are you empathetic? Do you have strong accountability?

Say that, instead. Ask others:

- What are three words that describe me?
- What am I really good at?

Create a draft statement using your key words and the feedback you received. Once you've drafted your message, practice it aloud. If it doesn't flow, edit until it feels natural.

Tell someone else. Practice your value statement on your partner, or a close friend. Ask for their feedback, make adjustments, and repeat.

The most important pieces of information to convey in your value statement is what you do best, and how you add value.

Navigating Career and Family

You're rarely going to achieve a 50/50 balance between work and family, day after day, week after week, year after year. The key is recognizing some weeks, or months, family will be your priority, and will require more of your attention.

Other times, things at work will require some sacrifice at home to pull a project or initiative through to completion. Having support from others and staying aligned with where you need to focus at the time is important to having a healthy mindset.

Work/life balance is a myth. Instead, we should strive to live *prioritized* lives. When your time aligns with current priorities, you will be more at peace. Trying to achieve a 50/50 balance leads to a flat-lined life. Sometimes current priorities require your all, but it should be for a defined time period, not prolonged.

At the beginning of the book I discussed the importance of values identification. Knowing your values and creating priority alignment between your focus and your values is important.

I am a mother of three (fourth on the way), balancing career and mom duties, sometimes masterfully, other times disasterfully and I've learned the single most important thing that has given me peace.

I have a witty, smart, thoughtful almost-19-year-old with a smile that melts my heart.

I have an equally intelligent, creative, and kind 15-year-old that still comes to hug me goodnight.

I have a firecracker daughter who is nearly three years old who is bilingual in Spanish, has hair like Shirley Temple, and loves to unload the dishwasher and eat dry cat food when I'm not looking.

And sometimes, defiantly, even when I am.

Like most mothers, I've had days where I cried the whole drive to work feeling guilty not being with my kids.

I've had days where I was thrilled to be working because of an exciting project that lit my fire, and I've had days where I wondered what the heck I was doing with my life, and feeling spread thinner than the spandex on my thighs when I was 9 months pregnant.

Through it all, in addition to my own struggles with guilt, I'd get input from well-meaning others.

Stay-at-home-moms sometimes, albeit unintentionally, made me feel I was *less than* because I traded field trips or homeschooling for a career.

During periods I was home with the kids working moms would say things like, "I give you credit. I could never stay at home because I need to be doing something with my brain."

Ouch!

The point is, as a mother I could never seem to make the right choices. My mind was my enemy no matter where I camped out. And the disapproving voices of others could never be satisfied.

That's just addressing the simple choice of work, or not-to-work. We won't even get into the judgment we place on each other in our parenting!

What I've learned is women aren't always a sister-hood. We're not always kind and supportive of each other. We judge each other.

We make ourselves feel better and try to silence our inner critic by telling ourselves we're doing it better than someone else.

The most important thing a mother can do is be kind. First, to yourself, and to other moms. We're all trying to do the best we can, and you never know the challenges each woman is facing.

The next time your inner voice criticizes you, or another mom, silence it.

We all need a little grace for the journey.

Final Thoughts

I hope this book has given you a lot to think about, ideas, and resources to start taking steps to find and follow your star. You don't have to eat the elephant all in one bite. Pick one new habit, implement one new technique.

Start a development plan document and add actions to take in the coming weeks and months. Use your calendar to schedule high important/low urgency activities that contribute to your goals.

Growth is a journey; it begins with one step.

Although the five success factors were defining in my mom's inspirational story, I would be remiss to omit a sixth factor at work: her support system.

Surround yourself with people who believe in you, encourage, and support you. My friend and colleague, Susan Whitcomb, calls these your "bone marrow people."

I leave you with these words from *The Great Escape*:

"Listen, he said, you ever seen a bunch of crabs in a bucket?

No, I told him.

Well, what happens is that now and then one crab will climb up on top of the others and begin to climb toward the top of the bucket, then, just as he's about to escape another crab grabs him and pulls him back down.

Really? I asked.

Really, he said, and this job is just like that. None of the others want anybody to get out of here. That's just the way it is in the postal service!

I believe you, I said.

Just then the supervisor walked up and said, you fellows were talking. There is no talking allowed on this job.

I had been there for eleven and one-half years.

I got up off my stool and climbed right up the supervisor and then I reached up and pulled myself right out of there.

It was so easy it was unbelievable. But none of the others followed me.

And after that, whenever I had crab legs I thought about that place.

I must have thought about that place maybe 5 or 6 times before I switched to lobster."

Charles Bukowski

All the best to you!

Appendix: Additional Tools & Resources

*R*eaders should be aware that internet sites mentioned as references or sources may have changed or no longer be available since this book was published. To download supporting resources for this book in one zip file, go to http://www.virtuscareers.com/Pages/Book. aspx

Life-long Learning

Coursera

www.coursera.org – Coursera offers high quality courses, many from accredited and reputed academic institutions. From business, data sciences, personal development, social sciences, computer sciences, and more, there's something for everyone to learn. Many courses are free, and some of the more in-depth programs and curriculum come with a nominal cost. For example, *High Impact Business Writing*, offered by the University of California, Irvine, is a mere $35 for 4-8 hours of content.

Mind Tools

www.mindtools.com – Mind tools is a monthly subscription services and offers high quality content in areas such as Leadership Skills, Communication Skills, Career Skills, Decision Making, Team Management, Creativity Tools, and much more.

At the time of this writing a Mind Tools subscription is $19/month. For $27/month you can access premium features, such as learning streams and expert interviews.

Alison

Alison.com also offers free online courses and certification through 400 different courses in 10 course categories. Launched in 2007, the site helps people earn certification in topics like legal studies, psychology, health studies, project management, and human resources. The content is free, but to get a copy of your certification it costs about $20 at the time of this writing.

Saylor Academy

Saylor.org offers free online courses. There aren't as many offerings as *coursera.org*, but the courses are all free.

Academic Earth

http://academicearth.org - Academic Earth curates a collection of free online courses from the world's top universities, using a platform to facilitate the global sharing of ideas. In addition to a comprehensive collection of free online college courses, Academic Earth features an ongoing series of original videos, including case studies that look at large, successful organizations. Finally, this site offers links to relevant trade journals.

Some courses include:

- Adaptive Path: Creating Meaning for Employees
- Advanced Managerial Communication
- Competitive Decision-Making and Negotiation
- Executive Education
- Individuals, Groups, and Organizations
- Innovation and Inertia
- Leadership at a Time of Transition and Turbulence
- Managing the Innovation Process
- Negotiations and Conflict Management
- Strategic HR Management

Open Education Database

http://oedb.org - Open Education Database (OEDB) offers an open courseware collection that includes thousands of free audio and visual lectures, full courses, and multimedia across all subjects.

They offer a wide array of courses, including:

- Behavior Modification
- Communication for Managers
- Fundamentals of Human Resources
- Fundamentals of Project Management
- Growth Strategies for Business
- How to Plan Your Career Path
- Innovation, Enterprise & Creativity
- Knowledge Synthesis for Career Development
- Preparing to Manage - Skills and Practices
- Professional Writing
- Selling Principles
- The Concept of Innovation
- What Great Leaders Do

Open Culture

http://www.openculture.com - Open Culture brings together high-quality cultural and educational media for the worldwide life-long learning community. Open Culture's mission is to centralize this content, curate it, and provide access to high-quality content whenever and wherever you want it.

This site offers free resources for over 800 online courses, including:

- Intro to Project Management
- Operations Management
- Managerial Accounting
- Introduction to Business Administration
- Writing for Strategic Communication
- Basic Concepts of Operating Systems & System Programming
- Technology & the Future: Managing Change and Innovation
- Discover Your Value
- Strategic Management
- Decision Skills: Power Tools to Build Your Life

Want to open a whole new world? Try learning a new language! Open Culture offers opportunities to learn **47 languages**, including Spanish, Chinese, French, and Russian.

Self-Awareness/Openness to Feedback

Competencies – Assessing

http://www.virtuscareers.com/Documents/Follow%20Your%20Star/Competency%20Self%20Assessment.docx

Competencies – Development
George Washington University – Learn Now: *https://ode.hr.gwu.edu/learn-now*

Emotional Intelligence Assessment (Free)
http://www.ihhp.com/free-eq-quiz/

Personality Strengths Exercise
Contemplate and identify your positive personality qualities
http://virtuscareers.com/Documents/Follow%20Your%20Star/Personality%20Strengths%20Exercise.pdf

Self-Awareness Assessment
http://insight.lominger.com/insight/sort-card.html
Strengths Identification
Discover your natural talents using StrengthsFinder. Only 1 in 33 million people share the same Top 5 strengths.
Cost: $15.00 for Top Five Strengths
https://www.gallupstrengthscenter.com/Purchase/en-US/Product?Path=Clifton%20StrengthsFinder

Strengths – Entrepreneurial
Perhaps you're interested in gauging your entrepreneurial potential. The Entrepreneurial Profile 10 is a cost effective way to evaluate your strengths for running your own business.
Cost: $12.00
https://www.gallupstrengthscenter.com/Purchase/en-US/Product?Path=Entrepreneurial%20StrengthsFinder

Values – Identifying and Prioritizing
An exercise to help you discover and rank your values
http://virtuscareers.com/Documents/Follow % 20Your % 20Star/ Identifying % 20Your % 20Values.pdf

VIA Character Strengths (free)
From the VIA Institute on Character: "Research tells us that individuals who use their character strengths lead happier, more satisfying lives. Only when you understand your unique character strengths can you begin to live a life that is engaging, exciting and rewarding to YOU."
Register to take the VIA Character Strengths Assessment here: *https://www.viacharacter.org/Survey/Account/Register*

WorkPlace Big Five Assessment
http://www.virtuscareers.com/Documents/Follow % 20Your % 20Star/ Introduction % 20to % 20the % 20WorkPlace % 20Big % 20Five % 20 Profile % 20Traits-Competencies.pdf
Contact ksherry@virtuscareers.com to receive an assessment of your workplace behaviors and competencies to assist with clarity on role fit, or for team-building for your organization. A student version, SchoolPlace Big Five, is also offered for teens and college students to determine best-fit academic and career pursuits.

Women's Inventory for Success Empowerment (WISE) Profile
The WISE Profile enables women to gain insights to help them navigate the challenges in their career so they can achieve

maximum career and leadership potential. No matter what stage a woman is in her career, this assessment will give her valuable awareness into her competency level on critical career and leadership success factors.

To understand your natural strengths, identify potential areas of growth, and understand what you can do to move forward in a powerful and confident way in your career, contact *ksherry@virtuscareers.com.* To become certified in the WISE assessment, contact Valerie McMurray of NorthStar Consulting Group, at *http:// www.thenorthstarcg.com/contact/.*

Building Strong Relationships

http://www.collaborationbreakthrough.com/ - This website has downloadable tools, blogs, and a companion book, *Collaboration Breakthrough,* to work more collaboratively with others.

Everything DiSC® Personality Assessments

For Senior Leaders: DiSC® Work of Leaders
Discover your approach to Creating a Vision, Building Alignment, and Championing Execution, with strategies to improve across these three critical areas for leaders.

Work of Leaders provides a simple three-step process to help you reflect on how you approach the most fundamental work of leaders: Creating a Vision, Building Alignment around that vision, and Championing Execution of the vision. Unlike other DiSC® reports, which emphasize understanding the differences between people, Work of Leaders focuses on understanding how your tendencies influence your effectiveness in specific leadership situations.

DiSC® Management

The DiSC® Management tool is an instrument designed to teach you how to bring out the best in employees and yourself. The management specific, personalized report helps you work more effectively in the areas of:

- Delegating and directing
- Motivating
- Developing others
- Working with your own manager

The DiSC® Management instrument increases your effectiveness using personalized learning to help you develop your management style, improve communication, and increase employee engagement.

DiSC® WorkPlace

For individual contributors:

- Gain insights into your own behavior and that of others
- Understand and appreciate the styles of the people you work with
- Learn how to make communication more effective
- Create strategies for overcoming challenges when working with people of different DiSC® styles

DiSC® Sales Profile

For anyone in, or aspiring to, a sales position:

- Understand Your DiSC® Sales Style
- Recognize and Understand Customer Buying Styles
- Adapt Your Sales Style to Your Customer's Buying Style

Visit *http://www.virtuscareers.com/contact-us* if you're interested in taking the DiSC personality assessment to help increase your interpersonal skills.

Effective Communication Skills

The *Communication Breakthrough Tool* by RV Rhodes, LLC: Learn simple, effective strategies to coach others, give feedback, and build agreement.
http://www.collaborationbreakthrough.com/free_stuff/Breakthrough%20Tools%20Conversations.pdf

The 7 C's of Communication: *https://www.mindtools.com/pages/article/newCS_85.htm*

Being a Risk Taker

- Move outside your comfort zone by setting stretch goals and seeking out challenges
- Grow your ability and knowledge to calculate the positives and negatives of taking chances/risks toward building your career
- Use this free **Risk Impact/Probability Tool** offered by MindTools® to work through risk, impact, and risk mitigation options to increase your probability of success

https://www.mindtools.com/pages/article/newPPM_78.htm

Miscellaneous Resources

Career Self-Assessment Exercise
Generate job role ideas by assessing desired work focus, work attributes, and job families
http://www.virtuscareers.com/Documents/Follow%20Your%20Star/Career%20Self-Assessment.pdf

26 Job Families
A reference for Career Discovery; view sample jobs within the 26 Job Families
http://www.virtuscareers.com/Documents/Follow%20Your%20Star/26%20Job%20Families.pdf

ACT World of Work Map
A tool to research job roles to determine the best career fit
https://www.act.org/content/dam/act/unsecured/multimedia/wwmap/world.html

Feasibility/Desirability Matrix
A decision-making tool to determine best career options
http://www.virtuscareers.com/Documents/Follow%20Your%20Star/Feasibility-Desirability%20Matrix.pdf

The Job Seeker Toolbox
Contains articles, tips and tools for Career Transition, Networking/Social Media, Salary Negotiation, Resumes, Job Search, Interview Preparation & Performance, Strengths (Discovering), and Personal Branding
http://www.virtuscareers.com/job-seeker-toolbox

Acknowledgements

First and foremost, to God, for gifting me with the talent, ability, passion, and purpose to help others discover meaningful work they are wired to do best, and the ability to write this book.

To my amazing husband Xander, who has supported my entrepreneurial calling in endless ways, from reading every career article I've ever written, to helping set up the technical "plumbing" of my business, to folding laundry and changing diapers when I was hammering away on my keyboard, and never complaining about my 8:00PM client calls. I love you forever, Xander.

To my funny, smart boys, Tristan and Justin, who have graciously allowed me to put them through endless assessments and actually listen to me when I coach them on their own future careers. Girls, you're next!

To my supportive parents who've helped mold me into the woman I am today and encouraged me to confidently rise to my potential by being my biggest cheerleaders.

To my incredible clients, without whom there would be no book to write. I've been honored to walk your professional journeys with you. Your victories are my victories. Your challenges are my challenges. I'm grateful for your business and your friendship.

To my dear friend Kimberly Tilley, who edited this book on her own time, and helped me with countless ideas in support of the book and Virtus Career Consulting.

To my brilliant mentor Steve Lishansky, President of Optimize International (and the unofficial Kristin Sherry fan club). You've helped me learn more about myself and to become, as you would say, an "Executive Coach Extraordinaire."

To my colleague and creator of the WISE profile, Valerie McMurray, thank you for introducing me to, and certifying me in, your fantastic, one-of-a-kind assessment for women.

To my colleague and mentor, Brian Ray, thank you for your hours of counsel and guidance when helping me name my company, this book, and for being a positive source of energy in my life!

To my friends and extended family, thank you for your words of support and enthusiasm while I was tackling this project. Your words of encouragement helped me keep pressing on toward the goal!

About the Author

Kristin Sherry is Founder of Virtus Career Consulting, guiding adults to discover and align their strengths to realize career fulfillment, teams to increase their effectiveness, and students to determine best fit academic and career pursuits.

Formerly, Kristin served as a Learning & Development leader at a Fortune 20 company where she managed the company's learning strategy and coached leaders and teams to increased effectiveness.

Kristin speaks at various forums on career-related topics and facilitates quarterly career workshops. She lives in North Carolina with her husband, Xander, and their children.

To contact Kristin, visit *www.VirtusCareers.com*.

A portion of the proceeds of this book will be donated to Crossroad's Career® Network, a non-profit public charity 501 (c) (3) organization which helps people find jobs, careers and God's calling. It is a national membership of church and community organizations, schools and colleges, and professional affiliates in coaching, counseling and consulting. They provide faith-based career and job search online resources combined with on-the-ground, and one-on-one help.

Notes

PART 2: First Things First

Why You're Here

[1] http://www.gallup.com/poll/165269/worldwide-employees-engaged-work.aspx

[2] http://www.frbsf.org/economic-research/files/wp09-11bk.pdf

Find Your Star

[3] Lombardo, M. & Eichinger, R. (2003). Leadership Architect Norms and Validity Report. Minneapolis: Lominger.

[4] Creativity Research Journal Copyright 2004 by 2004, Vol. 16, No. 1, 1–9

Career Transition

[5] Lessons about Career Change: https://www.youtube.com/watch?v=NKwYTmHExWQ

PART 3: The Five Success Strategies

Success Strategy # 1: Self-Awareness/Openness to Feedback

[6] http://greenpeakpartners.com/resources/pdf/6%208%20 10%20Executive%20study%20GP%20commentary%20 article_Final.pdf

[7] Emotional Intelligence: https://en.wikipedia.org/wiki/ Emotional_intelligence

[8] Law of Concentration and Law of Becoming: http://blog. iqmatrix.com/negative-mental-attitude

Success Strategy # 3: Building Strong Relationships

[9] OneBrick.org provides support to local non-profit and community organizations by creating a flexible volunteer environment for those interested in making a difference in the community.

Success Strategy # 4: Life-long Learning

[10] Carol Dweck, The Power of Yet: https://youtu.be/J-swZaKN2Ic

Success Strategy # 5: Being a Risk Taker

[11] Crossroads Career® Workbook © 2011-2012

[12] Allan Watts: What if Money Were No Object: https://www. youtube.com/watch?v=yNqvXiUNe2o

Part 4: Bonus Success Superchargers

[13] Critical Thinking in Everyday Life: 9 Strategies http://www.criticalthinking.org/pages/critical-thinking-in-everyday-life-9-strategies/512

[14] https://www.ted.com/talks/shawn_achor_the_happy_secret_to_better_work/transcript?language=en

Follow Kristin on Social Media!
Twitter: @Virtus_Careers
LinkedIn: www.linkedin.com/in/kristinsherry

Book Kristin for Speaking Engagements
http://www.virtuscareers.com/contact-us
Conferences and Key Notes
Corporate Team Builders & Events
Networking Events
Workshops
Podcasts

www.ingramcontent.com/pod-product-compliance
Lightning Source LLC
Chambersburg PA
CBHW031533040426

42445CB00010B/513